Fire in the Morning

NIALL O'DOWD is the editor and founder of *Irish Voice* newspaper and *Irish America* magazine, the two leading Irish American publications. He is considered a leading authority on the Irish American community and the Irish Diaspora and has appeared on *Good Morning America, NBC Today,* CNN and *The Charlie Rose* show on PBS. He continues to be a frequent analyst for CNN on Irish issues. In addition he has written many opinion pieces published in the *New York Times, Washington Post* and *The Irish Times* on Irish American issues. He was awarded the American Book Award by the Before Columbus Foundation in 1996 for "excellence in writing." An arts graduate of University College Dublin and a native of Tipperary, Ireland, he moved to the US in 1978. He started his first publishing venture, a monthly Irish American magazine, the following year in San Francisco. He moved to New York in 1985 and founded *Irish America* magazine that same year and *Irish Voice* in 1987. He also founded the Top 100 *Irish America* Magazine Awards, held every year at the Plaza Hotel. Jim Dwyer, Pulitzer Prize winner and *New York Times* writer has called O'Dowd "the authentic voice of the Irish in America." He is a resident of Manhattan and married to Debbie McGoldrick; they have a daughter, Alana.

For Alana

NIALL O'DOWD

FIRE in the
MORNING

The story of the Irish and the Twin Towers on September 11

A Brandon Original Paperback

First published in 2002 by
Brandon
an imprint of Mount Eagle Publications
Dingle, Co. Kerry, Ireland

10 9 8 7 6 5 4 3 2 1

ISBN 0 86322 298 6

Cover design: Lyn Davies | Design
Typesetting by Red Barn Publishing, Skeagh, Skibbereen
Printed by ßetaprint, Dublin

CONTENTS

CHAPTER ONE

INSIDE GROUND ZERO

"THREE BODY BAGS at West and Broadway, immediately." The female police dispatcher could not be more clinical. It is obvious she is having plenty of practice in bringing out the dead.

A moment later the walkie-talkie crackles again: "Body bag at West and Fourth." Then a pause: "Fireman."

Thanks to a friendly police captain, I am one of the few outsiders who has entered Ground Zero, the area near Wall Street which took the full impact. It is just three days after the devastating attack.

For the purposes of the visit I am a construction worker. A fellow journalist and myself had arrived for the rendezvous at Ground Zero hopelessly overdressed, the police captain told us. We had gone to my friend's hotel so he could dress down, and then we had driven to my apartment where I had donned a baseball cap, sturdy Doc Martins, a T-shirt and a pair of blue jeans.

The trepidation I feel is like nothing I have ever experienced. While the events of 11 September were horrific, somehow watching them on television like the rest of the world cushioned the impact. On the upper East Side, where my apartment was, the only immediate impact was a vast cloud of smoke and dust in the distance, lazily floating out towards Queens.

Almost every person interviewed likened it to a horror movie set. Perhaps subconsciously that was where I, too, had consigned it, finding it hard to understand it in the light of harsh reality.

Now, however, the full impact of the worst attack ever on American soil was about to be laid bare. At Ground Zero there would be no place to hide or to fantasise that it was just a bad movie.

On the way down we quickly realise we are entering a war zone. There is the incredible sight of armoured personnel carriers once you move into the lower Manhattan area. Everywhere there are army units, and the sight of hundreds of men in army fatigues against a New York backdrop is deeply incongruous.

Overhead we occasionally hear the screech of the F16s as they patrol the skies over the city. A palpable air of menace still hangs over everything as they fly over. Until the drone of the engine disappears, every plane is another possible attack. New York has become a white-knuckle city, 8 million people on edge wondering what will happen next.

Where once you could drive down the FDR Drive and admire the soaring vistas around Wall Street, now there is only an acrid smoke which envelops every building and every living thing like a London smog. The smell is like burning rubber, but there is something else that smells bad in the air, too. "You'll be needing these, lads," says the police captain, handing us face masks. He's right. Within minutes the white cotton begins to turn darker with almost every breath.

You could still kid yourself that it is a normal Manhattan Saturday morning, albeit one with almost no traffic on the FDR Drive, until you hit the first checkpoint with heavily armed soldiers, shotguns at the ready, peering at every car.

We are a few blocks from Ground Zero, still on the East Side of Manhattan, and we intend to drive past the Staten Island ferry location and loop around the bottom of the drive until we approach the Ground Zero site. My escort flashes his police badge and is waved through several checkpoints. The soldiers were jumpy, ill at ease, and there is no banter or small talk.

The police captain tells us that earlier that day the chief of police, Bernard Kerrick, had read out the names of the dead policemen and women for the first time. "It's fairly tight," he says, using a police term for something shocking. "I knew many of them."

We park the police car and begin walking through the haze in the direction of Ground Zero. Every few yards we have to step over lines of cables from the emergency generators. The din of men and machines at the pile makes hearing any conversations difficult.

Off to our left the West Side Highway is completely buried under a sea of rubble. The pedestrian bridge that spanned it has collapsed, and the highway looks like a picture of London during the Blitz.

Soon Ground Zero comes into sight. The immediate impression is of a massive, stricken animal stretched on a funeral pyre. It is much bigger than it appears on television, almost three blocks long and 70 feet high, a complete tangle of metal, concrete, steel and debris. Heavy fumes of smoke arise out of the pyre, and our escort tells us that fires are still raging below the surface.

This is now all that remains of the twin towers, the 1,350-feet tall fingers in the sky over Manhattan which occupied a sprawling 16 acres. Strangely, a line from a Shakespearean sonnet comes to mind: "Bare ruined choirs, where late the sweet birds sang."

The outside of the World Trade Center had a particular tan colour, unseen elsewhere on skyscrapers in Manhattan. During my last visit to the towers, two months before, I had noticed this distinctive colour for the first time. Now huge slabs of tan-coloured rubble from the towers lie in ruins all around me.

To walk around the site takes the best part of an hour. We move from west to east and then south to north. Everywhere is covered in a pale white dust, ankle deep in spots, which sticks to your clothes and at some places makes breathing difficult. Several times we stop to cough and to clear our lungs.

Roadblocks every few yards are manned by heavily armed National Guardsmen and regular army, who make it clear they will brook no argument if they stop you. Other security forces, armed with shotguns, guard many of the entrances to the site. Many have guard dogs, too, who are on full alert. Fortunately our police escort is able to wave us through, but even he gets his credentials checked at an FBI checkpoint.

We walk by the ruined Marriott Hotel, formerly the Vista, one of downtown Manhattan's most popular places for both tourists and the after-hour Wall Street crowd. The bar in the hotel was always full of intrigue as Wall Street singles congregated in large numbers after the final trading bell, and matches were made and lost in the hazy glow of cigarette smoke and low lights.

Because it lay at the base of the twin towers, it has been completely destroyed. When it was known as the Vista, in 1993, it rose out of the ashes of the terrorist explosion that year to assume its former glory. It will not succeed in doing that on this occasion.

On a nearby building a massive American flag has been pinned by workmen who scrambled up a huge crane in order to hang it. All around on every available space are hastily scrawled messages of love and support for those who were lost, and the ubiquitous "United We Stand." Incongruously, one message scratched in dust says *"Tiocfaidh ar lá"*, the old Irish Republican catch-cry.

The World Financial Center, too, has suffered greatly. Beside it, the prestigious Manhattan Yacht Club harbour, where the sleek ships of wealthy Wall Streeters once moored, is now jammed with tugboats and barges taking rubble away. It was from the Yacht Club that three firemen requisitioned an American flag and placed it on an adjacent flagpole. The photograph of them hanging it has now gone down as one of the most indelible images in American history.

The narrow streets we are traversing as we walk around the huge pile are dust and debris strewn. At Gino's Pizza parlour, a tattered menu still clings to a sandwich board. Near by, at O'Hara's Irish Pub, covered in white dust, an Irish tricolour hangs limply.

There are asthma stations and makeshift medical stations at several points. In many places, exhausted workers sleep where they have fallen, stretched out on hard concrete, surrounded by dust and debris. The most distressed are the firefighters, many of whom just stare at the ground during their breaks, neither eating nor drinking. The full impact of losing 343 of their colleagues has begun to fully sink in.

On top of the wreckage, from every vantage point, like little ants, thousands of rescue workers try desperately to pry the steel beams apart, to shear off the massive concrete columns and continue the search for their missing comrades and civilians.

The ironworkers are the undoubted stars of the rescue effort. When the pile shifts, all others run for their lives, but not the ironworkers. "When the rubble shakes, everybody runs except them," says the police captain with an admiring shake of his head.

At ground level, workers were passing back buckets of debris by hand in an ever-lengthening chain that seems to stretch for miles. The men barely glance up, their faces grim and determined. They know that every second is vital if more survivors are to be found. They know, too, that it is fast becoming a long shot.

Police officers, firefighters, FBI men, construction workers are all working furiously in what is becoming a losing race against time.

They have removed 22,000 tons of debris in just over four days, an extraordinary achievement. Unfortunately there are an estimated one million tons left. The heroic efforts to date have succeeded in shifting less than 2 per cent of the wreckage.

Every so often workers in a certain spot pause, and a body bag is called for. The firemen rush in to see if it is one of their colleagues. Suddenly there is complete silence, with no machinery running or voices shouting above the din while the body is respectfully removed. Then the grim business begins again.

What is perhaps the most distressing sight are the fire engines, which had been lined up on the West Side Highway and took the full force of the debris from the imploding buildings. Many of the vehicles have now been lifted by cranes and set down in a vast storage yard, one on top of the other, waiting for disposal. There are many other cars and police vehicles there, all flattened like pancakes in this grave-yard, but it is the fire engines that draw the eye. You hope no one was in them or underneath them when the debris field hit, but you know there has to have been. You could quite comfortably fit what is left of them in the storage area of a few large trucks.

Somewhere underneath all this rubble of Ground Zero are the 343 firemen. One of their colleagues put it in per-spective for me. "In 150 years, since the fire service was founded, we have lost 700 men. In one day we have lost half that amount." It is a shocking figure, but when you see the fire trucks, which took the full impact of the falling build-ings, you understand why.

A fireman tells me that one of the eeriest sounds of all is mobile phones and pagers still ringing underneath the wreck-age as loved ones still frantically try to find those missing.

On a 1-acre site not far from Ground Zero is the Irish Famine Memorial, still under construction. The gable end of what will be a replica of a nineteenth-century Irish cottage has just been completed with stones shipped from Mayo. Workmen heard the planes go overhead on the day, and some saw the impact on the nearby Trade Center. They con-sider themselves lucky to be alive. Suddenly the Irish Famine Memorial does not appear as important to me as it was just a few days before.

It is estimated that one-third of those dead lost their lives trying to save others. The Bible says it all: "No greater love can a man have than to lay down his life for his friend." Or in this case, a stranger. It is estimated that over a thousand did so on 11 September, between police, firemen, emergency workers, fire wardens in the different companies, security personnel in the two towers and civilians who stopped to help others who were trying to exit the buildings. It is a roll of honour like no other in American history.

CHAPTER TWO

RIDERS ON THE STORM

UNITED FLIGHT 175, a Boeing 767 non-stop from Boston's Logan Airport to Los Angeles with seven flight attendants and 56 passengers on board, rolled back from Gate 19 shortly after 7.45 a.m. on 11 September. The captain was Victor J. Saracini, 51, a native of Pennsylvania. The first officer was Glen Horrocks, 38, also of Pennsylvania.

Ruth Clifford McCourt, 45, and her four-year-old daughter Juliana were among the passengers. A native of Ireland, Ruth was an extremely successful businesswoman who had created a Boston beauty spa that drew customers from all over Europe and the US. She was also strikingly beautiful. Tall, blond and elegant, Ruth was perfectly dressed for every occasion.

Juliana was a duplicate of her mother, with angelic good looks and a mischievous smile. At a wedding just the week before, Juliana had played with the other children. Afterwards one of the mothers told Ruth that her daughter had said she'd been "playing with an angel", meaning Juliana.

Despite her business success, after the birth of her daughter in 1997 Ruth became a full-time mother, devoted to the blond little girl who was the centre of her and her husband David's life. She had recently returned from a trip to Portugal with Juliana and was excited because the little girl had learned to ride her pony on her own.

Originally from Cork, where her father, a paper merchant, was a leading figure in business, Ruth, the only girl among five children, left for America with her mother at age sixteen when her parents separated. After college she began working for Barbizon, an institute for learning about cosmetics that has outlets all over the United States. Her territory was in the South, in the Birmingham, Alabama, area.

She became a skincare specialist, training in one of London's top schools. When she returned to the US in 1986, she opened her own spa, Clifford Classique, in the Newton area, a suburb of Boston. It was an immediate success.

In 1995 she met David McCourt, twelve years her senior, a businessman from a wealthy Connecticut family that traced its roots back to Waterford. McCourt had inherited his father's gas distribution business, and he and his brother had expanded it greatly. Ruth and David met through tennis-playing friends. It was love at first sight, and within six months they were making plans to get hitched.

The wedding at the Vatican was a bittersweet affair, however. Five days before the ceremony, Valentine, Ruth's beloved father, had passed away. He had just finished writing his speech for her wedding. The family decided to go ahead with the wedding anyway.

In typical fashion, Ruth had wangled an audience with the pope for her and her new husband. She had promised an influential priest in her district that she would set up a meeting with Katharine Hepburn, a family friend, if he returned the favour with the pope. "Done!" he'd said.

Now she was flying to a Deepak Chopra seminar on the West Coast. She was a devotee of the New Age guru, as was Paige Hackel, 46, her close friend who was travelling on American Airlines Flight 11, leaving at about the same time to go to Los Angeles. They had not travelled together because they had different frequent flyer programmes.

The friends had spent the previous night at Paige's house, planning their trip, which would end with a visit to Disneyland in Anaheim, California, for Juliana.

In the car on the way to the airport, Juliana's orange juice had spilled out of its container in Ruth's handbag. The driver remembers that Ruth took it all in stride, her well-known ability to remain calm during crises great and small showing itself. The driver remembers an excited trio, laughing and chatting as they prepared for their long trip.

Also on board the United flight that Ruth and Juliana were on was Marwan al-Shehi, a citizen of the United Arab Emirates who had recently attended flight school in Florida, and five other men from the Middle East: Fayez Ahmed Hassan, Ali Banihammad, Mohand Alsehri, Ahmed Alghamadi and Mamza Alghamadi. All the men were dressed in khakis and tan tennis shirts, not unusual for a flight that would terminate in sunny California. Surprisingly, none of the men had any carry-on baggage.

American Airlines Flight 11, with Paige Hackel on board, had departed at 8.04, ten minutes before the United flight. On board were Mohammad Atta, an Egyptian with flying experience, and four other Middle Eastern men who all sat in first class.

The two planes began climbing to their scheduled altitude of 36,000 feet. At 8.37 a.m. the first sign that something was amiss came when the United flight received an unusual request from the tower asking if they could see the American flight.

"Affirmative, we have him, he looks about 29, 28,000 feet," responded Captain Saracini. At 8.41, the United pilot, obviously now concerned about the American Airlines plane, reported, "We heard a suspicious transmission on our departure from BOS," using the airport's three-letter code. "Sounds like someone keyed the mike and said, 'Everyone remain in your seats.' "

Air traffic control began to scramble. Over Albany, New York, the American Airlines flight took a sharp left and headed due south towards New York City, well off its flight path. Then came a chilling transmission from flight attendant Amy Sweeney. She told a flight services manager at American that five hijackers were on board. She described them as being of Middle Eastern descent and stated they had stabbed two of the fight attendants. "A hijacker cut the throat of a business-class passenger," she said, "and he appears to be dead. They have just gained access to the cockpit."

At 8.43 United Flight 175 also veered from its flight path over northern New Jersey. It continued south for a brief period before making a U-turn towards New York City.

The nightmare had begun.

Soon after he awoke, Ruth McCourt's brother, Ron Clifford, 47, heard the sound of his phone ringing in his Glen Ridge, New Jersey, home. It was his breakfast appointment, asking him if they could switch from the Marriott on Times Square to the one at the World Trade Center. He looked at his watch; it was 6.30, and the World Trade Center was actually closer than the midtown destination. Quickly he agreed.

This was a very important appointment. Ron's software company, Tradewind Net Access, specialising in e-learning, was about to close a major deal over breakfast, he hoped. As his sister Ruth had suggested, he dressed in his dark blue suit, white shirt and yellow silk tie. Ruth had told him to be sure to wear a matching hanky in the breast pocket. "You have to stand out," she'd said.

It was a beautiful sunny day and his daughter Monica's birthday. Coincidentally, she would be 11 on 11 September. He planned to come home early to help her celebrate.

He gazed out at the azure sky, a perfect autumn day, and decided to take the train across from New Jersey, then the ferry from Hoboken to lower Manhattan, rather than drive. That would give him time to walk around the World Trade Center. As an architect, he was endlessly fascinated with the building's extraordinary structure, and when out-of-towners visited, his guided tour of Manhattan usually ended at the twin towers.

In fact, the week before, when preparing to sail off Manhattan, a minor problem with the shaft of his boat had put him in contact through a friend with an engineer named Bob Devillas, who had just retired as the chief engineer at the World Trade Center in charge of ventilation and heating. As Bob fixed the shaft, they chatted about his previous job. In the 1993 bombing carried out by Arab militants, in which six people were killed, he was the first person into the basement after the bomb went off.

Ron called a neighbour close to the station to find out

the train timetable. The New Jersey PATH train would leave at 7.30 sharp. He would make it easily.

When he reached the Hoboken ferry, he marvelled again at the beauty of the day. During the short hop across the Hudson to the pier, he found himself praying that his meeting would go well. He and his Indonesian partner were on the verge of greatly expanding their software company. Today's breakfast meeting would be a vital step forward.

Because he used to work in the vicinity of the World Trade Center, Ron knew the area well. He got off the ferry and walked the few blocks to the Marriott. He knew there had been major renovations to the old Vista Hotel since the change in ownership – the architect in him wanted to see the connecting lobby to the World Trade Center. It was 8.30 and he had 30 minutes to fill before the breakfast.

Inside he walked down the marble hallway of the Marriott and into the World Trade Center lobby, a place of soaring ceilings, dramatic light and incredible hustle and buzz. He always found it stark and very dramatic. He lingered, then was heading back through the connecting revolving door when a massive explosion rocked the building. It was 8.46 a.m.

American Flight 11, travelling at 494 miles per hour with hijacker Mohammed Atta at the controls, had hit the north tower between the 94th and 99th floor, exploding on impact, its 24,000 gallons of jet fuel creating a mighty fireball. On board was Paige Hackel, Ron's sister's best friend, and the woman he spent every New Year's with.

"I remember that I smelt paraffin right away. I didn't equate it with aviation fuel, and I immediately thought that it must have been a tank rupture in the basement," he says.

Suddenly the building began to shake and secondary explosions could be heard. All around him people began screaming and running. He made towards the connecting doors with the Marriott Hotel.

Then he saw a woman walking out of the haze towards him. Her hands and her body were completely burnt. She was walking like Frankenstein with her arms directly in front of her because her arms were so swollen. Her face was unrecognisable, her head was bare of any hair. A hair slide was burnt into her skin. He knew immediately she was in desperate shape. She had been waiting for a bus outside the building and had run inside when a fireball had engulfed her.

"The man who was next to me is dead," she told Ron.

"I told her to sit down and I ran into the bathroom and looked around and found a plastic bag that I filled with water," Clifford remembers. It never occurred to him to just leave the woman. "That's not my way, not the way of my religion," the staunch Catholic says. "I doused her with the bag of water, then I screamed repeatedly for help. I stood up, kept my eyes on her and shouted for EMS support."

Suddenly the woman spoke. "Jesus, Sacred Heart of Mary, help me," she said. Ron knelt down next to her, knowing now she was a Catholic, and they said a Hail Mary and then the Lord's Prayer. Then a woman arrived with an oxygen canister and they had her breathe from it.

She told him her name was Jennieann and asked him not to call her mother, who she said was too frail and ill to be told about her daughter's condition. She gave him her boss's name at Paine Webber brokerage house and told him she was allergic to latex and was an asthmatic. He scribbled all the details down on a notepad he found in her bag.

At this point he could hear the building shaking and groaning. Because of his architect's training, he was listening for the harmonic convergence, the vibrations coming from the building indicating how it was handling the stress and strain. He did not like what he was hearing. Then came the second massive explosion. Overhead, United Flight 175, travelling at 586 miles per hour, carrying his sister Ruth and his beloved niece Juliana, slammed into the south tower between the 78th and 84th floor with incredible force. He had no idea they were on board and actually thought they had left for California a day or so before.

"I knew we had to get out of the building," he says, and he got Jennieann to her feet and asked her if she could make it. "She told me yes, so we commenced moving. I was screaming at the top of my lungs for people to get out of the way. They were so horrified when they saw her that they parted like the Red Sea. Somebody shouted, 'It's a plane.' Someone else, 'It's two planes.' Then it finally struck me what had happened."

Because all her clothes had been burnt off, a black waiter gave Clifford a large tablecloth to cover the stricken woman. Eventually they made it outside.

"It was pure carnage," he says. Every couple of moments there was a loud explosion like a bomb, which he realised was the sound of people hitting the ground after jumping from the top floors. Cars, trucks and buses were ablaze or burnt out altogether. There were bodies on the street everywhere.

"The noise, that's what I remember most," he says now, "the awful noise and panic."

Huge girders crashed down from the buildings on to the Plaza, and the bodies kept falling. "There is stuff I saw that I will have to deal with for the rest of my life," he says.

Suddenly, out of the smoke and gloom a fireman appeared. "Run for your life," he screamed at them. "Run, run, run."

Then Ron saw the most extraordinary sight of all: dozens of firemen rushing towards the death trap, going into the building he had just left in order to save people. "I've never seen such bravery," he says now.

He crossed over the West Side Highway to the line of ambulances that were drawn up. Tenderly, he helped Jennieann to the first on the line. "You have to make it now, after all we have been through," he told her. After Jennieann was taken away, Ron turned and saw young men on the upper floors skydiving off the building. He saw one couple holding hands as they fell. Everywhere a thick cover of ash and soot was descending on the living and the dead. It was sheer hell.

He made his way to a public phone in a nearby building, miraculously still working, and called his wife Bridget. She had been watching CNN when the story hit. Sick with worry, she had been trying desperately to reach him on his cell phone but all service was out.

"I'm okay," he told her. "I've just gone through hell, but I'm okay." His next call was to his sister Ruth, who he thought might pick up her cell phone. There was no answer. He hardly gave it a second thought.

As he spoke, bodies were still falling in front of the window of the building he was in. He said to a man near to him, "These buildings are coming down." The man said no, that he was an engineer and that the trade towers could withstand even airplanes crashing into them. He remembers thinking the guy must know what he was talking about.

He remembered also that New Jersey Transit had recently announced that in the event of any emergency, trains would line up at the arrival point on the Jersey shore of the Manhattan ferries to bring people to safety. He walked to the nearby South Ferry landing and waited to board. All that was on his mind now was that he had to get home to his family.

Hundreds were waiting along with him. Women and men were on their knees praying. The sound of police and fire sirens filled the air. He was afraid they would lock down the area before he could get out.

Luckily he managed to get on board a ferry, and he remembers standing with a woman from Northern Ireland when they saw the south tower collapse in a massive plume of smoke. "This can't be happening," he told himself over and over.

Ron jumped on the first train, and a man with a Blackberry pager told everyone that Washington, too, was under attack. He thought the world might very well end that day.

The train dropped him one station from his house. Finally he made it home, bedraggled, exhausted, the burnt skin of Jennieann on his shirt and suit, his tie covered in aviation fuel. He desperately wanted to take a shower to clean up.

Just as he stepped into the bathroom, Ruth's husband David called with undisguised concern in his voice. He thought, but he wasn't sure, that Ruth might have been on one of the flights. Ron remembers a sinking feeling and thinking, "Oh shit, this just can't be."

For the next several hours he worked the Internet, calling up the United and American web sites. He found out from

Paige Hackel's husband Alan that he had been with Paige and Ruth the night before and that a driver had picked them up that morning to drop them at their separate terminals. "I had dinner with two of the most beautiful and vivacious women in the world last night, and now they're gone," he told Ron tearfully.

Ron still had not given up hope, but as the hours passed and he began to fully put the pieces together he knew it didn't look good. "We're in trouble," he told Ruth's husband. "Jesus Christ, this can't be happening."

Finally, confirmation of the passenger list came from the airlines. Ruth, Juliana and Paige were all gone.

"When it was finally confirmed, I was numb, totally numb," says Ron. "My brothers in Cork had been so relieved that I escaped, none of us originally thought that Ruth was involved. Then it all came out."

He often thinks of those last moments of his sister and niece, wondering what they went through. "I think Ruth probably exemplified calmness – she would have talked to Juliana, read to her, they might even have sung a song together. She was no panicker; she was trying to control whatever she could, telling her daughter everything was fine. It wouldn't surprise me if she had a calming impact on her fellow passengers around her, too."

After 11 September, Ron says he functioned on false energy for weeks, communicating news to his family (Ruth's body was not found until January, Juliana's has not been found) and arranging a memorial service in Connecticut at the beach house that Juliana, Ruth and David had called home. Over 1,200 showed up at the church. Seven hundred people attended the reception and the last song was "Galway Bay", one of Ruth's favourites.

A few days after the memorial, Ron Clifford stood at the bedside of Jennieann Maffeo, the woman he had helped on the morning of 11 September. Maffeo, a 38-year-old computer analyst with Paine Webber, lived in Brooklyn with her sister Andrea and her elderly parents from Italy. Now she was in the burns unit at Cornell Hospital on Manhattan's East Side, one of the best in the world, but the nature of her horrific injuries meant it was long odds that Jennieann, now unconscious, could survive.

With him Ron Clifford brought his yellow silk tie, the one his sister Juliana had recommended he wear for his important breakfast. It was now stained with aviation fuel, and he placed it gently beside Jennieann's bed as a token of the experience they had had together. Then he lowered his head and prayed for the young woman who had so randomly come into his life under tragic circumstances. He pleaded with her to make it, to defy the odds, to make some good happen out of a horrible experience.

Her parents and sister, he found out, had been desperately looking for her after the Trade Center buildings came down, and her boss had eventually called them after he got the information Ron had written down. Jennieann had asked Ron not to call her mother because she was frail and elderly; now the family was carrying on a vigil 24 hours a day beside her bed.

Her father embraced Ron like a son and kissed him profusely, thanking him in heavily accented English for giving him his daughter back, no matter how briefly.

Forty days after she had been terribly burned, Jennieann gave up her fight for life. Ron had just dropped off his brothers, who had come over to see Ground Zero, to the airport. On the Van Wyck Expressway on the way back home from Kennedy Airport, the news of her death came over the car radio. Ron pulled over and cried his eyes out. He later received a personal letter from President George W. Bush, sympathising with his loss and commending him on his bravery in trying to save Jennieann.

He went to the wake in an old Italian neighbourhood in the shadow of the Verrazano Bridge. It was very emotional, he remembers, huge bouquets of flowers from Paine Webber where Jennieann had worked, and friends, relatives, acquaintances all breaking down in tears.

After the memorials, Ron fell apart. Totally drained, he suffered from post-traumatic stress. Luckily, he knew to go to the right people, and slowly his confidence has returned.

Still it was difficult. When showering he found himself

continuously scraping his feet to the point where they almost bled. His therapist told him that he was reliving the scene from outside the World Trade Center where he walked on the ashes of the dead. Ron remembered a scene from *Schindler's List*, the movie about the Jewish Holocaust, that was similar to what he experienced, and suddenly he understood.

He says he's not angry at Osama bin Laden, and given his Christian forgiveness it is no surprise. He is sad, however, that people can be so misguided that they think they can come closer to God by killing other human beings.

Now his main priority is to make his business even more successful, and then to commit to the Juliana Fund, a non-profit organisation he has started up to promote tolerance and understanding in children. He feels that that is what Ruth and Juliana would have wanted.

Then, on a January weekend, Ruth's husband David called to say that they had found some of Ruth's belongings and that he was going to collect them. When he got there, the FBI handed David a sealed plastic bag containing Ruth's Hermes handbag.

Overcome, David went back to his hotel room before he opened it. Inside, eerily, he found a World Trade Center ID card. Ruth had visited an estate planner and lawyer in the World Trade Center, one recommended by Ron, the previous June to discuss her and David's affairs.

There was also a papal medal commemorating her wedding at the Vatican, damp and musty credit cards and a burnt and bent driver's licence. David gave the bag to Ron, who took it home and placed it on a countertop in his house. He felt that Ruth and Juliana's spirit pervaded the room after he did so. In a strange way, he felt that they had come home to him.

CHAPTER THREE

A LOVE STORY

O N THE DAYS when he left the New York Public Library in midtown Manhattan for his lunch break, Patrick Day would blow a kiss in the direction of the twin towers where his fiancée, Ann Marie McHugh, worked.

Ann Marie joked that she was so high up she could never see the kiss because the clouds obscured her view. But she appreciated the gesture anyway, which she thought was in keeping with the hopelessly romantic nature of her husband-to-be.

They were going to be married on 24 November in Florence, Italy, on Thanksgiving weekend. Patrick, who had a masters in art history, and Ann Marie, who had studied art in college in Ireland, were looking forward to indulging one of their favourite pastimes by strolling through the marvellous Florentine galleries during their honeymoon.

The tickets for Florence were safely tucked in a drawer beside their bed at home. They had considered Ireland, where Ann Marie's parents lived, as a location for their marriage, but the complications of shipping Patrick's relatives from South Dakota and other points west was too great, they reckoned. Why not do it quietly in a city they both felt inspired by?

They had planned a big family after they came back to New York. They had already agreed names for the children: Caitlín, Áine or Shannon for girls, Brian, Patrick or John Patrick for boys. They had checked when they were most likely to achieve pregnancy after their honeymoon. Pat, 37, and Ann Marie, 35, wanted to get on with the business of a family as soon as possible.

On one recent night Ann Marie had told him that she could not stand to lose a child and that she would feel her life was over if it ever happened to them. Patrick told her he would rather not have a family if that were the case, because he couldn't stand the thought of losing her.

They had got engaged in 1999, just one year after they had started dating. Patrick's family had an unusual tradition where the eldest male in the family inherited the engagement ring that his father had bestowed on his mother. On the night they got engaged, however, Patrick did not have time to have the ring sent to him from South Dakota, so he got a temporary replacement, ordered up an expensive bottle of wine, cooked her favourite dinner and then, with his heart in his mouth, proposed. She accepted.

His wife-to-be had been born on the upper East Side of Manhattan at Lennox Hill Hospital to parents from Tuam, County Galway, on 15 April 1966. Soon after, the family had left New York and ended up back in Ireland in Tuam, where her father Mike opened up a bar and restaurant.

Though she was brought up in Ireland from an early age, Ann Marie never forgot her American roots. Thus, it was no great surprise when she arrived back in her native city in the summer of 1985, a fresh-faced 19-year-old, anxious to pick up the threads of her American life.

She began working at Aer Lingus, but soon she moved to the financial district, on Wall Street, first as a secretary. Later she took the audacious step for a woman of seeking her own stockbroker qualification so she could work in the intense, male-dominated world of high finance.

She was a natural. Despite never having gone to any formal classes, she scored one of the top marks in the City Seven exams, as the entrée to the brokerage business is called. Having started as a secretary at Cantor FitzGerald, a massive Wall Street firm specialising in government bonds, she was one of the few people in company history to switch to the trading side of the desk.

"She could do 14 things at once," says Patrick now, when asked about his fiancée's particular talent. Often, when he visited her, he would watch, fascinated, as she conducted several different conversations, bid on different securities and continued to talk to him at the same time. She even found time, he remembers, to straighten out other people's deals; and in the testosterone-charged world of wheeling and dealing, she more than held her own.

She was so good, in fact, that the lead broker at the firm hired her as his key aide, a job she performed to his complete satisfaction, despite the fact that he had fired the three previous occupants in quick order.

She was with Cantor Fitzgerald for 12½ years, working on the 104th floor of the World Trade Center in the north tower. Often she and Patrick would have lunch at Windows on the World on the 107th floor, with its stunning vistas of New York City. It was one of their favourite things to do, to walk up the stairwell from Cantor to the Windows on the World.

Ann Marie knew the stairwells well. In 1993 when the World Trade Center had been bombed by terrorists, she had walked all the way down from the 104th floor to safety. She remembered how calm everyone had been at the time.

In 1999 she had been headhunted by Eurobrokers, a new company set up in opposition to Cantor, who had offices on the 84th floor of the south tower. Eurobrokers had recruited 15 of the best from Cantor Fitzgerald, and she was among the first chosen. Every morning around 7 a.m. a staff car would pick her up outside their apartment and take her down to the World Trade Center; a half hour or so later Patrick would get up, shower, and walk to his job on Fifth Avenue at 42nd Street.

Life was often hectic for her, carrying out complicated trades, wooing prospective clients, staying competitive, always keeping an eye on competitors anxious for a share of the multi-billion-dollar government securities business.

It was a long way from the Tuam childhood and the quiet backwater she grew up in in the West of Ireland. But she loved the life and the pace of everything. She also found time to relax in their cosy fifth-floor, one-bedroom apartment on the upper East Side, not far from FitzPatrick's Pub on 85th and Second, where much of their social life took place.

She was also a complete sports nut, and one of the happiest days she and Patrick spent together had been on 1 September 2001, when they watched Ireland beat Holland to make qualification for the World Cup in 2002 almost inevitable. They had watched the game in Fiona's Bar and Restaurant on First Avenue at 86th Street with a bunch of their friends from Ireland, and the celebrations lasted long into the night. They joined in the singing of "Olé Olé Olé", and there was even talk of trips to South Korea or Japan for the finals proper.

She also retained an undying love for the sports teams of her home county, Galway. On 9 September, early on Sunday morning, she had dragged Patrick off to watch the All-Ireland hurling finals, also at Fiona's, live from Croke Park. They watched in sadness as Galway lost both the minor All-Ireland final and the senior game for a double blow to the county.

After the games, Patrick had insisted that they stay and watch his beloved Minnesota Vikings in the National Football League. As a South Dakota boy, the Vikings from nearby Minneapolis were as close to a hometown team as they had.

He matched her passion for Galway with a love for the New York Yankees, an unusual choice for a Midwesterner but one that he has fiercely defended all his life. Indeed, he was such a fan that when he first started going out with Ann Marie she had put up with him placing an earpiece in one ear to listen to the games while talking to her at the same time. "She was the first woman who accepted my madness for the Yankees," he remembers with a smile. "It meant a lot to me at the time."

She would often call him at work because he had no access to television or radio and tell him from the TVs on the trading floors how the Yankees' afternoon games were going. He planned to host his bachelor party at a Yankees' game. The date was set for 10 September, the same night his idol,

Roger Clements, known universally as "the Rocket", was pitching.

Supporting the New York Yankees was not the only aberration that made Patrick Day different from many of his contemporaries growing up. Though born in South Bend, Indiana, he had moved to the outskirts of Yankton, South Dakota, when just a child. His parents both taught at the University of South Dakota, his father John a dean of the college in fine arts, his mother Fran a biochemist. Yankton, on the banks of the Missouri River, had been settled primarily by German, Swedish and Norwegian immigrants, attracted by the vast tracts of land available and not fazed by the harsh winters. Patrick Day, actually born on St Patrick's Day in 1964, was one of the few Irish around; and he, his parents and his sister Julianne made sure they celebrated St Patrick's Day every year.

After high school he went to the University of South Dakota, then on to the University of Minnesota in St Paul, specialising in art history, anthropology and history, eventually getting a master's degree in his field.

In 1997 he moved to New York to commence studying for his doctorate at New York University. He took a job working at the famed New York Public Library designing museum exhibits and growing increasingly close to his Irish roots. He also began bartending at night in FitzPatrick's and soon had a ready circle of friends, mostly from Ireland, who hung out at the bar.

Ann Marie came into his life in August of 1999. He literally bumped into her on the street; she was going with a mutual friend to see a movie and they asked him along. The friend left after the film, and Patrick and Ann Marie walked together through Central Park, through the FAO Schwarz legendary toy store on 60th and Fifth Avenue and stopped at a couple of Irish bars. They talked as if they were old friends and were immediately very easy in each other's company. It was love at first sight. "From the day I met her, we were only three days apart," Patrick remembers.

On 10 September Patrick went with his best man, a fellow South Dakotan living in Connecticut, to the Yankees' game to see Clements pitching. By any standards it was a tiny bachelor party, and Patrick guessed his friends had planned something larger closer to the time. He wasn't really into the bawdy beer and bachelor party scene, however. The Yankees with Clements aiming to become one of the fastest 20-game winners in history was just fine for him. The fact that the Boston Red Socks, the hated rival of the Yankees and Clements' former club, were the opposition got him even more hyped up for the game.

The best-laid schemes, however, sometimes end in disappointment. It was a rainy New York evening, so wet in fact that the game could not start. Patrick was not too miffed at first, however, as he and his friend were secure from the elements under an overhang, and the beer and hot dogs tasted good.

Amazingly, just two rows behind him was a young Irishman in a Tipperary hurling jersey, the team that had beaten Ann Marie's beloved Galway in the All-Ireland hurling final the day before. They kidded back and forth about it.

As the evening shadows fell and the hard rain continued, it became evident that the game would not be played, much to Patrick's disappointment. On his way back to Manhattan, he wondered if he should call Ann Marie or not, as he was coming home much earlier than expected. However, she was tired from their long outing the day before watching the games at Fiona's pub and he decided to leave her alone. Besides, she had told him to stop off in FitzPatrick's on the way home to say hello to a friend of hers, Philomena Nolan.

Once in the warm atmosphere of his local, the thought crossed his mind again to call Ann Marie. He thought they might make a night of it, a bachelor party celebrated with his wife-to-be. Then they could sleep in the next morning, on Tuesday, 11 September, and spend the day finishing the wedding invitations they had been trying to complete for the past few weeks. Again he thought better of it.

He didn't realise until he got home that she had been awake, making calls and preparing wedding invitations. She would have been glad to join him, she said, and the "bachelor party" might have been considerably enlivened.

That night Patrick found it difficult to sleep. Too many hot dogs eaten during the rain delay followed by a few drinks led him to wake up several times with indigestion. He remembers that every time he woke up, Ann Marie and he were holding hands. He knew they were both tired, and he decided after one sleepless bout he would not wake her if she slept through her alarm and that he'd call in sick for her.

Tuesday, 11 September, dawned bright and balmy, perhaps the nicest day of late summer in the city. The alarm clock woke Ann Marie, much to Patrick's chagrin, and she stepped into the shower. When she came out they talked about the disappointment of missing the Roger Clements game the night before and the possibility of going that night, 11 September.

It depended on his friend, whether he had to get back to Connecticut or whether he could stay over on their couch another night. Patrick still had half a mind to skip work, hang out with his friend and go to the ballpark that evening.

They made their bed together, she teasing him about not getting to work on time and warning him not to fall back asleep. At just after 7 o'clock her car service arrived and they kissed goodbye at the door. The car would take her down the East Side to the tip of Manhattan, cross over by the Staten Island ferry building and drop her outside the World Trade Center well in time for an 8 a.m. start.

Patrick showered, walked to work and was sipping his first cup of coffee of the day when he called her at about 8.20 that morning. He was in the basement of the public library working on a project; she was high on the 84th floor of the south tower of the World Trade Center.

From her window she had an uninterrupted view of the north tower, and suddenly, around 8.45, she interrupted him in mid-sentence and said urgently, "Something has hit the building, there's stuff everywhere, I gotta go." Patrick believes that from her vantage point she could see that an explosion had hit the other tower, but she couldn't see that it was a plane.

At first Patrick thought she might have said she had got hit on a bid, using brokerage terminology, but he remembered distinctly he had heard her say the building was hit.

Immediately concerned, Patrick called back, but Ann Marie had left and a stranger answered the phone. He called again and talked to a friend, Paul, who told him, "It's not us, it's the other building. I think Annie has left."

What exactly happened to Ann Marie McHugh after she left the 84th floor will likely always remain a mystery. Based on her 1993 experience, she had clearly decided to evacuate quickly, and she certainly had enough time to make it to safety. Almost every one of her fellow workers who left later survived, including two who even stopped to go the bathroom before they left.

When she began her descent on the stairwell, there was no general commotion, and making it to the ground should have been possible. One woman later told Patrick that Ann Marie had saved her life, staying with her when she was panicking and reassuring her. There were several reports that she was busy keeping everyone walking down the stairwell calm, telling jokes and reassuring them that she had been there in 1993 and that she had walked out safely, as had almost everybody then. The last place she was reported was at the 40th floor where the elevators from the higher floors terminated and the ones to the ground floor began.

Did she decide to take one of the doomed elevators at that point? As an asthma sufferer, she may have had shortness of breath. Perhaps a fireball had come crashing down through the elevator shafts and engulfed her and others. One possible report had her outside the building being helped by a police officer.

Patrick Day does not know what happened, except that nobody can say for certain. He stayed at his desk at the New York Public Library, desperately hoping she would call. He called his best man at his apartment and told him to stay by the phone. He e-mailed and called her frantic parents, family members and friends in Ireland, and told them he was waiting to hear. The silence from the phones was ominous. He ran to a security guard station in the library and watched horrified as the two towers fell.

Finally he determined that he would take the subway down there, but by the time he reached the station all service had been cancelled. As he crossed Fifth Avenue where he usually impulsively blew a kiss to his beloved towards the looming twin towers, now he saw with a sense of profound shock that they were no longer there. There was only a massive cloud of dust and debris which was slowly inching its way uptown and towards him.

He walked to his apartment, numbed by the horrific events. For hours he pictured her coming home all covered in dust and grime from the explosion, but there was no key turning in the lock. He desperately scanned the television video of the crowds now streaming uptown, hoping to catch a glimpse of her. There was no sign.

As hope began to fade, he clung to the belief that she had been injured and was lying unidentified in one of the hospitals where victims had been brought. A desperate search of emergency rooms, however, revealed nothing.

He stayed home and waited. He did not sleep for several days, staying awake watching television, hoping desperately to see her on footage somehow, somewhere. Reality did not set in right away; he still waited and hoped that somehow she would turn up, injured but alive.

His friends and his family kept him going. His parents were amazed, coming from South Dakota, to find such a sense of community in the huge impersonal city they had imagined New York to be. His apartment was overrun with people, everyone hoping against hope that survivors would be found among the rubble, that somehow, against all odds, Ann Marie would make it through.

It was not to be. His beloved Ann Marie was gone, her body not found. "Sure I cry sometimes, but it was a privilege to know her," he says now. "I lie down and cry, then I think of something funny we did and I laugh. She's still here. Half of her went to me when we met, and half of me to her when we met.

"I don't dwell on the hatred towards those who did this. I wanted spend my energy in a positive way. There are days I am very angry, but life is not about that. It's about what Ann and I talked about, being married, having kids, and spending our lives together.

"Our planned wedding day, 24 November, was tough, no question about it. It was what we were living for, but my friends have been very special. They have made sure I have been taken care of as much as possible."

He travelled to Ireland for a memorial service for Ann Marie in her beloved Galway. It was a healing occasion for him. "People know how to deal with grief there; there's an understanding and a depth that is really impressive."

Ann Marie's heartbroken parents joined him for Christmas in New York. A photo of their lost daughter adorned the dinner table on Christmas Day. They are, he says, "very special people" who will "always be in my life. This has come as such a blow to them."

His toughest day was when he received her death certificate and it listed her as single. "Even though it meant nothing to other people, it meant a lot to me," he says. "I wish it said we were married, that it showed that she was loved as much as she was. She deserved that."

CHAPTER FOUR

THE FIRST ATTACK

MAHMUD ABOUHALIMA WAS unusual-looking for an Egyptian. He had red hair and a red bushy beard and freckles. He was 6 foot 2 inches tall and extremely well built. On this day, 26 February 1993, just after midday in lower Manhattan, he was also hoping to witness a particularly evil kind of history.

As he made his way through the bustling downtown crowd to J and R Music, a great sprawling megastore selling everything from classics to rock to country, the former New York cab driver knew exactly where he was going. Once upon a time he had been a jihad fighter, braving the Soviet troops in Afghanistan. After that war, fought with American money and materiel, he had helped remove Soviet mines from the ruined fields.

That campaign had ended but holy war had not. He was the advance guard of a new war, this one fought in America's cities and streets and anywhere American influence could be found. He, Mahmud, was about to help strike a major blow for Allah.

Once he reached J and R's, he quickly made his way to the second floor and the classical music annex. He stood at the window facing south, his back to the massive Mozart collection, over eight hundred records in all. As the soothing music played on, he ignored it, fixing his gaze on the World Trade Center towers looming in the near distance. He waited.

Just 11 days earlier, a compatriot had gunned down two CIA employees in Langley, Virginia. It was the first blow of an anticipated double whammy, and the killer had escaped scot-free and fled to Afghanistan.

Two and a half years previously, Mahmud had been the wheel man when Rabbi Meir Kahane, a Jewish right wing radical, had been assassinated in a Manhattan hotel. Mahmud had screwed up. He was looking for a parking spot when the deed was done, and the killer had jumped into the wrong cab and been easily caught. Mahmud was sure he and his compatriots would get this one right.

At exactly the same time as Mahmud positioned himself at the window, two men in a rented Ryder truck entered the parking lot deep in the bowels of the World Trade Center's north tower. In the truck was a 1,500-pound bomb which had been mixed in a huge vat in a storage locker in Jersey City.

Once the two men had parked the car, they produced a lighter and placed it against the fuses. Then they departed in a red back-up car which had followed the truck to its parking spot.

At 12.17 the burning fuse reached the blasting cap. It was the moment Mahmud was waiting for, the second when the north tower would topple on to the south tower and leave tens of thousands dead in the ensuing carnage. As the explosion swelled and rocked the music store, Mahmud smiled.

TOBIN'S FOLLY

The twin towers, the tallest buildings in the world when they were completed, were the brainchild of Austin J. Tobin, a first-generation Irish American who headed the Port Authority for much of his 45 years with the company. In a contemporary account, Tobin was described as "a small and solid man with a full head of silver-gray hair, handsome and clean shaven with a square jaw, always wearing a conservative blue-gray, two button, single breasted suit". He retired a broken man in 1971.

Every morning Tobin came to work in a chauffeured Cadillac from his apartment on the upper West Side near Central Park. When he arrived at work, the elevator operator, previously warned, slipped on a pair of white gloves as he accompanied the director to his executive office on the 15th floor of the Port Authority building on Eight Avenue on the West Side. From his eyrie Tobin had an unrivalled view of the Hudson River and several of the bridges and tunnels between Manhattan and New Jersey that his Authority presided over.

As late as 1900 there were no bridges from New Jersey to New York, and Manhattan, Staten Island and New Jersey were unconnected except by boat. Part of the reason was the political rivalry between New York and New Jersey, with the latter in the role of the unappreciated country cousin. During the First World War, however, the lack of proper transportation severely hampered the movement of war supplies. Finally shamed into cooperating, the two states created the Port Authority.

Established in 1921, the Port Authority was charged with building and maintaining bridges and tunnels into New York from all directions. It was given unlimited political, financial and human resources at a time when the best and the brightest went into public service rather than Wall Street.

Soon the Port Authority had amassed vast wealth and huge political power, and when the Holland Tunnel, the first link between New Jersey and New York, was completed in 1924, the success of the Port Authority was evident. The tunnel was immediately financially successful, as the number of registered automobiles in the US increased enormously, jumping from 8 million to 27 million in a few years.

Soon after came the Outerbridge Crossing linking New Jersey and Staten Island, the George Washington Bridge, the Midtown tunnel and many other projects.

In 1942 the Port Authority promoted one of its brightest young stars, Austin Tobin, then 39, to head up the agency. A Holy Cross College graduate, Tobin had also gone to Fordham Law School, the classic route for the child of Irish immigrants, and he wrote poetry on the side. Once he took over the job, he worked seven days a week and completely devoted his life to the Port Authority.

Soon after he took over, with the Second World War over and the country flushed with the fruits of victory, a can-do spirit prevailed across America. It was then that the idea of a World Trade Center, set up to capitalise on the brave new world of international trading across boundaries, time zones and continents, was born. Austin Tobin was the prime force behind it.

There were many hold-ups in the ensuing years, and it was not until 1960 that a specific design was finally drawn up. In March 1961 the Port Authority went public with their plans for the first time. Reaction was mixed, with many editorial writers saying it was an expensive waste of time. Crucially, however, *The New York Times* supported it.

In February 1962, Tobin created the World Trade Office, which had as its prime goal, building the World Trade Center. He appointed a close associate, Guy Tozzoli, an engineer, to plan the job.

The decision to locate on the West Side on a 16-acre site was taken. Two hundred and eighty commercial tenants, 43 industrial tenants, more than 1,000 offices of various sizes and 100 residential tenants had to be displaced. A fierce battle to preserve the neighbourhood ensued.

The Port Authority prevailed, however. Soon, using Tobin's unrivalled political connections, they signed up the US Customs Service and the State of New York as anchor tenants for the new wonder building. President John F. Kennedy, egged on by Tobin, gave the project a surprise boost when he called for its completion during a visit to New York.

The architect was a surprising choice, Minoru Yamasaki, a Japanese American born in Seattle. His job was to create a structure that would house 50,000 workers and would have 100,000 daily business visitors. When completed it would be the size of a major American town.

Tozzoli and Tobin, anxious to create a stir about the new

building, told Yamasaki that they wanted the tallest building in the world, a title then held by their Manhattan neighbour, the Empire State Building, which is 105 storeys high.

In January 1964 the Port Authority announced its plans to spend $350 million on two 110-storey towers with a joint capacity of 10 million square feet of office space. Tobin had to go into public relations overdrive to combat the critics, who thought it was a wasteful, environmentally insensitive white elephant. By early 1966 Tobin had finally overcome all the objections.

The World Trade Center buildings had an unimpressive start, with no public groundbreaking or media fanfare. Instead, nine men from the Ajax Demolition Company armed with crowbars and sledges began to smash up a five-storey building at 98 Dey Street on 21 March 1966.

On 17 August Tobin faced a major crisis when US Steel and Bethlehem Steel, the big two suppliers, issued bids that were 50 per cent higher than expected. In a bold move, Tobin cut them out of the project altogether, much to their chagrin.

The requirements for the project were awesome: 1.2 million cubic feet of earth and boulders would have to be removed, as well as 45,000 feet of bedrock. Half the site would be where the Hudson River used to be, and the builders would have to drill down to that bedrock, some 70 feet beneath the ground.

The material requirements were mind-boggling: 200,000 tons of structural steel, 15,200 feet of wire, 400 miles of conduit and 20,000 lighting fixtures would be used. In addition, workers would install 7 million square feet of acoustical tile and 7 million square feet of floors.

In December 1966, Tobin was forced to announce that the cost of building the towers had skyrocketed to $575 million. Critics began derisively calling the project "Tobin's Folly". Undaunted he pressed on.

During the building of the twin towers the structural engineer, Leslie Robertson, felt that wind, not explosions, was the greatest danger. "The energy input from hurricane force winds acting over 110 stories high far exceeds the energy from aircraft impact or bomb," he wrote.

The towers were designed to ensure that they could withstand winds of up to 150 miles an hour, an unheard of occurrence in New York, but the planners were taking no chances. In March 1980 during a gale the tops of the towers actually moved a total of eight feet.

However, in a prescient moment, Robertson also allowed for the possibility of an explosion. "Sabotage of perimeter buildings was considered to be an expected event in the life of the building," he wrote decades before his nightmare scenario came true.

Over the next few years the towers' construction continued to cause controversy. A major debate over worker safety on the site was sparked after several horrific injuries. Featherbedding by union workers was alleged, with lurid stories of men earning over $100,000 a year, a massive sum at the time.

Then the first-ever report showing that asbestos caused cancer was released, and the Environmental Protection Agency issued a new set of standards concerning the spraying of asbestos materials. Spraying had already reached the 35th floor, and it took a massive effort to remove the asbestos and respray with a new and safer compound.

By late 1970, however, the project was entering the home stretch. On Monday, 19 October, a single piece of steel measuring 36 feet high was hoisted into place to complete the 103rd floor. The Empire State Building at 1,250 feet high was now eclipsed, by four feet, by the new tallest building in the world.

The twin towers would eventually stand 1,350 feet high, but its reign as tallest building would be short-lived. In Chicago, the Sears company was preparing to build a structure measuring 1,450 feet. Known as the Sears Tower, it still stands today as the tallest building in America.

On Monday, 19 July 1971, Austin Tobin was present to see the south tower topped out and the building essentially completed, though the official dedication ceremony did not take place until April 1973 when it was fully ready for occupancy.

That Monday in July was a grey, raw day, and it reflected Tobin's mood. He had become increasingly discouraged by the fierce internecine fighting in the Authority and the rush for glory by every politician in New York and New Jersey to claim credit for the new building. In December 1971, worn out by the controversies, Tobin announced his retirement, the great work of his life just completed.

At the official ceremony in 1973, Austin Tobin was nowhere to be found among the crush of politicians, including the secretary of labour and the governors of New York and New Jersey. The excuse he gave was that "it was raining".

Four years later, in 1977, terminally ill with cancer, Austin Tobin's last wish was to be taken down to the site of his beloved twin towers one more time. His long-time aide, Guy Tozzoli, did the honours. He stated afterwards: "It was his dying wish. He had me take him down in a wheelchair, and he sat alone looking at the Plaza and the twin towers for about two hours. True, he was a lawyer and a great executive, but in his heart he was an architect. He loved architecture."

On 8 February 1978, Austin Tobin died at his Manhattan home. In 1982 the Port Authority named the plaza in front of the buildings the Austin J. Tobin Plaza. At the time it seemed a fitting memorial.

A LUCKY ESCAPE

The explosion on 26 February 1993 hit the World Trade Center like an earthquake. The explosion left a crater the size of a four-storey building in the basement and almost ripped open the wall that held back the Hudson River. The impact of the explosion, however, bounced off the base of the north tower and gouged the huge crater in the nearby underground parking garages. A building that had been designed to withstand a major hurricane, however, did not buckle, even under what the FBI called the "largest improvised explosive device that we've ever seen".

The explosion would cost $300 million to repair and $225 million to clear all of the 110 floors of the soot and grime it created. Miraculously, only seven people, all working in the bowels of the building, were killed. Monica Rodriguez Smith, who was expecting a son, Edward, was perhaps the most tragic case.

But the building held firm. The north tower, which took the bulk of the explosion, never toppled like Mahmud Abouhalima had hoped. Worse for the Egyptian was the fact that in the rubble investigators found a key piece of evidence that led them right to the bombers: the identification number of the Ryder truck they used.

On 24 March 1994, four Islamic fundamentalists, including Abouhalima, were sentenced and jailed for life. It seemed a close run thing, but the twin towers had seemingly escaped the worst.

CHAPTER FIVE

A CLEAR MORNING

11 SEPTEMBER 2001 started like just another day. It was a beautiful autumnal morning in New York, the clear blue sky still holding a hint of summer and the crisp air a welcome respite from the dog days of August just passed.

Around the city, life went on in its usual way. The children were back in school after Labor Day, which meant there was far more traffic to navigate. The television news programmes were trumpeting the return of Michael Jordan, the greatest ever to play the game, back to the basketball court. It was actually such a slow week that a sports story led the nation's news.

Sport had been a frequent fill-in for real news. Venus Williams, the new US Open tennis champ, appeared on the NBC *Today Show*. In local sport, the tabloids announced the New York Mets had to win every one of their remaining games to make a play-off spot.

Meanwhile, in entertainment news, A.J. McClean of the boy band the Backstreet Boys was a major guest on *Good Morning America* to talk about a new release. The top movie of the weekend was *The Musketeer*, with a $10.3 million gross.

New York 1, the 24-hour cable news channel for the city, was running with the tale of the grand jury deliberating the fate of Lizzie Grubmann, the celebrity publicist who had allegedly backed her car into a crowd of customers outside a

Long Island nightclub after being refused entrance. On cable talk shows the Gary Condit case was all the rage. The California congressman was fighting off allegations that he was involved in the disappearance of Chandra Levy, an intern who worked in his office. For months on end the cable talk shows were "all Condit all the time", to quote one newspaper account. Now as summer turned to autumn the case had long since run out of steam, but was still leading the gabfests because of a lack of anything else to talk about.

The New York Times headline was dense: "Key Leaders Talk of Possible Deal to Revive the Economy. Bush is Under Pressure."

That week the Daily News had led with "Kips Bay Tenants Say We've Got Killer Mold", the New York Post with "City Divided as Vallone, Ferrer Trade Barbs over Race", a reference to the mayoral contest and the Democratic primary. Newsweek magazine was leading with "Shark Attacks" after a spate of such incidents on the East Coast, while Time was focusing on the slowing economy and its impact on consumers.

On the morning of 11 September, the city's mayoral runoff race wasn't attracting much attention. The polls opened at 7 a.m., but early indications were that the numbers of those showing up to vote were very light. Instead of lines snaking down the sidewalk before work, voters could stroll right in and cast their ballots in quick time.

It was easy to see why. On the Democratic side it had been a yawn of a campaign until the last week, with Public Advocate Mark Green leading the pack from the drop of the flag. On the Republican side billionaire Michael Bloomberg was expected to easily shake off the challenge of the perennial candidate Herman Badillo. Already there was speculation that he would spend up to $50 million trying to get elected. It was a bonanza for every political consultant and public relations expert in town.

The 43rd president, George W. Bush, wasn't making much news either on this Tuesday morning. According to The New York Times, his advisers were worried that he looked somehow too small for the massive job he had undertaken as president of the United States. The polls showed the country still deeply split after the debacle in Florida the previous November, with over half of Americans convinced that the Supreme Court of the United States had thrown the election unfairly to Bush.

Bush's cabinet seemed underwhelming also. Vice President Dick Cheney seemed likely to be felled by yet another heart attack at any moment. Many questions were being asked as to why Bush chose him in the first place when his health was so poor.

Secretary of State Colin Powell wasn't faring much better. He had even drawn a derisory cover in *Newsweek* magazine, wondering where he had disappeared to. It was clear he was the loser to the hardline hawks in the administration who opposed his moderate policies.

Meanwhile Secretary of Defence Donald Rumsfeld was widely viewed as over the hill and perhaps too tired for the job. Attorney General John Ashcroft had got the job only after a bitterly contested nomination fight and was still viewed with deep suspicion by leaders in the Democratic Party. No one could remember a more partisan time in American politics, other than after the resignation of Richard Nixon.

This day Bush was back in Florida talking about his education initiative. It was a workaday trip, mainly ignored in the media. Bush was to address a group of grade school students and read them a story. The betting was that it would be *The Very Hungry Caterpillar*, which opponents joked was the only book he had ever read anyway.

Back in New York, in hundreds of firehouses across the city, one shift was giving way to another, as the workers commenced their 24-hour workday. It had been a quiet night; the shift captains citywide reported nothing more troublesome than a few apartment fires which had been quickly extinguished.

Many of the men were still mourning their three colleagues, John Downing, Brian Fahey and Harry Ford. The men had been on duty on the afternoon of 17 June when a call came in about a spreading fire in Queens.

It had been Father's Day, and Fahey had been listening to an Irish radio programme on the Fordham University station hoping to hear a request for the Three Irish Tenors. John Downing had been packed to go for a month-long trip to Ireland, first to his wife's relatives in Kilkeel, County Down, then to his mother's native county of Kerry. Harry Ford had been a proud member of the Emerald Society of the fire department of New York.

A paint store in Astoria, Queens, had gone ablaze after two neighbourhood kids spilled some gasoline which ran into the store's basement and ignited a fire. The three firefighters had been killed in a massive explosion as they moved in to fight it. The deaths sent shock waves throughout a city no longer accustomed to losing their people in uniform, whether police or firefighters, due to far better safety regulations and a massive decrease in crime. Still, "Any given day a firefighter does not know if it will be his last,"said Kevin Gallagher, president of the Uniformed Firefighters' Association.

For the firemen themselves the deaths had a major impact. In Rescue Company No. 4 firehouse on Queens Boulevard in Queens, a chunk of wall from the collapsed building had been placed as a shrine to those who were lost. Near by, in Ladder 163, a similar chunk rested as a mute testimony to the men who had lost their lives.

At Downing's funeral twenty of his relatives from Ireland were in attendance. Mayor Rudy Giuliani swore, "We will never forget this hero."

Before Harry Ford's funeral the firefighters had gathered in Shines' in Long Beach, Long Island. The men explained to a reporter that it was an Irish tradition to drink and laugh at the funeral of a fallen firefighter. "We laugh when we shouldn't," Patrick McGlaughlin told *The New York Times*. "That's the way we deal with it. We know sometime, not too far away, we'll be back, and it will be one of us."

Firemen call each other Jake, especially at funerals where always there are out-of-towners they will not know. They explained their job to a reporter thus: "When the rats are running out we are running in. Not the brightest profession in the world, is it, Jake?"

Behind the bar a sign read: "Help Wanted. No Irish Need Apply." "If that rule were applied, Jake," said one fireman, "we'd all be out of a job here."

Now there were plans afoot to have a huge benefit for the men at Rory Dolan's bar in the Bronx. Several firefighters from around the city and even the suburbs had been pitching in to make it an occasion to remember. Cherish the Ladies, a very popular local group, were to headline. Bally Mac, Seanachaí, the Cunningham brothers, Eileen Ivers and other well-known local musicians were also to perform. The buzz on the street was that up to $300,000 might be raised. An anonymous donor had pledged $50,000 in matching funds. The money would go to the children of the firemen for an educational fund.

A "Benefit for the Bravest" was how one newspaper tagged it. Separately the *New York Post* fireman's fund had raised a million dollars for the families. Fireman Tommy O'Connor, one of the main organisers of the Irish benefit, said, "I'd just hope that if, God forbid, something happened to me, someone would look after my wife and children."

The benefit would never be held. At 8.45 that morning the entire world changed for ever.

CHAPTER SIX

IN THE BEGINNING

WHEN THE CRUSADERS sought to capture the Holy Land over 1,000 years ago, the local Muslim defenders, known as the Saracens, introduced a new and deadly weapon.

As the crusaders sought to advance on a walled city, the Saracens flung glass containers loaded with a highly flammable substance at them from the heights. Then they fired flaming torches which ignited the substance, resulting in horrific scenes of hundreds of men being burned alive.

Other crusaders, seeing their plight, tried desperately to douse the flames, risking their lives to save burning comrades. They were the first firemen in a sense, and many displayed incredible courage. Their heroism was rewarded by their fellow crusaders, who awarded each a badge of honour, a cross which became known as the Maltese Cross after the subsequent homeland of the Knights of St John, who were part of the crusades.

A thousand years later, the men of the fire department of New York all wear the same symbol as those given to the Knights of St John. When they went in to battle the deadliest blaze in American history at the World Trade Center towers on 11 September 2001, the Maltese cross was inscribed on each of their uniforms as their official badge.

In an eerie coincidence, the enemy they were facing was also an Islamic one, who had chosen to use fire as its weapon of destruction, in this case the white-hot heat of an exploding airplane and the jet fuel it spewed.

Like the knights before them, the firemen were braving the inferno to save their fellow man. Hundreds of them died. In the 350-year history of firefighting in New York, there had never been such an awful day.

CHAPTER SEVEN

THE FIRE DEPARTMENT

T HE FIREFIGHTING SERVICE in New York City was founded under the Dutch colonial rulers in 1648. The first firemen were equipped with 250 leather buckets made by Dutch shoemakers. They also had hooks and ladders and a system of fire watches, with eight wardens on duty at all times.

In 1731, the colony, now under the control of the British, had its first major advance in firefighting; hand-drawn pumps were brought all the way from London. All able-bodied citizens were required to respond to fire emergencies.

Following the War of Independence, the fire department was reconstituted as the Fire Department of New York, an all-volunteer force; but that was soon to change as the need for a full-time fire service became evident, especially during the Civil War.

The introduction of the steam engine was the final blow for the all-volunteer force, as firefighting now became a highly skilled profession that demanded full-time attention.

By 1865 the department had 552 officers and firemen. They worked seven days a week with one day off per month and three hours off for meals. Still there were many disastrous fires, and in 1866 the department was completely reorganised along military lines, which led to a far greater professionalism.

The history of the Irish in the fire department started in earnest around this time. Arriving immigrants were prime candidates for the fire service. Like the police service, it offered permanent work and reasonable conditions.

As Denis Smith, a former firefighter turned writer, has pointed out, in the first ten years after the creation of the paid department, five of the 20 firefighters who were killed were Irish. From 1865 to 1905, of the 100 firefighters who died, 66 were Irish. Seventeen of the first 23 fire commissioners were Irish, as were 13 of the first 17 heads of department.

On New Year's Day, 1898, the consolidation of all the boroughs of New York into a unified command meant the beginning of a new era for the fire department. The roots of the modern force of over 11,400 firefighters, 2,800 emergency medical technicians and 1,200 civilian employees date to this period. Today they serve over 8 million people in the New York five-borough area.

The New York fire department has remained an Irish bastion. In fact, 92 per cent of the force are Catholic, with those of Irish and Italian roots forming the overwhelming majority of the firefighters.

CHAPTER EIGHT

IN THE FOOTPRINTS OF ST FRANCIS

ON 28 JUNE 2000, Father Mychal Judge, a Franciscan friar, began walking from Dundalk in County Louth in the Irish republic to Belfast in Northern Ireland. He was accompanying Officer Steven McDonald, the hero New York cop, the third trip they had taken together there.

On previous visits they had met Taoiseach Bertie Ahern and other leading politicians North and South, who had encouraged them to continue with their peace work.

McDonald had been shot and paralysed from the neck down in 1986 while questioning three youths in Central Park. At the time he was 29 years old, married less than a year to Patti, who was two months pregnant. His subsequent story of survival, forgiving his shooter and becoming a great advocate for peace and reconciliation around the world has made him an icon in America.

"People know me from my act of forgiveness," says McDonald. "Father Mike and John Cardinal O'Connor were the two who most helped me understand the message of forgiveness. When I was called to forgive, it was their message and homilies that helped me understand to love my fellow man."

McDonald and Judge were in Ireland to publicise McDonald's efforts on behalf of peace, entitled Project Reconciliation. The idea was to walk the entire road to Belfast, about 50 miles, and to spread their message along the way.

Since the traumatic events that had almost taken McDonald's life, Judge had become a constant companion and almost a second father to McDonald's son Conor. His wife Patti called Judge their "best friend". MacDonald called him "a living face of Christ".

"We were a family," McDonald remembers. "He [Judge] often said to Patti Ann, 'It's the four of us . . .' There were good days and bad days. We disagreed on some things; we were disappointed with one another at times. But he would always end his phone call by saying, 'I love you.' "

They had met when McDonald was lying grievously ill in the hospital after the shooting and Judge was one of the priests assigned to him. McDonald attributed much of his recovery from his dreadful wounds, both mental and spiritual, to Judge's continuous help and understanding.

Judge also inspired his peace work and was anxious to visit Ireland again to help further that message. Now they had arrived together in their ancestral homeland. Father Judge had received his Irish passport in 2000 and had told McDonald that it was one of the happiest moments of his life.

On a previous visit in 1998 when they had gone to Omagh, site of the worse atrocity of the Northern Irish troubles, the town was still shaken by the horrific event; and McDonald remembers Judge meeting with family and friends of victims and consoling them for their loss. "People just gravitated to him," says McDonald. "You had to see it to believe it."

Now as they set off on their first steps towards the border town of Newry, a group called Kids for Peace surrounded them, singing as they marched and carrying a banner entitled "Journey to Forgiveness".

McDonald had many appointments along the way with politicians, self-help groups, victims of the Troubles, disabled police officers and the Orange Order, but the children singing moved them most of all.

The kids sang in the towns they passed along the way, and several other children approached them. One, a six-year-old, recited a poem about spring, a 13-year-old boy sang a song about peace that his mother had written.

Mike Judge was in his element in Ireland. He was, as a fellow cleric, Reverend Keith Fournier, remarked, "A priest and a pilgrim . . . spreading a message of love and reconciliation."

The group met with the Catholic Garvaghy Road residents in Portadown just before the annual furore over the attempts by the Orange Order to march down their road, which always drew world attention.

"We walked up Garvaghy Road," McDonald recalls. "The British soldiers checked us for bombs, and once we were cleared we were allowed to walk along it."

Remarkably, on the other side they went to Drumcree Church where the Orange march began, and they met with the Reverend John Pickering and Orange leaders. "There were men, protesters, outside, and they had weapons on them. I was physically shielded from this. They shouted at Father Mike, 'We don't allow people like you here.' They were threatening him, and he was in his Franciscan habit. Father Mike just looked at them and smiled." Then McDonald told his inspirational story of overcoming hatred and preached reconciliation, even in the most hard-bitten Orange neighbourhood in Northern Ireland.

They went back to the United States deeply fulfilled. Not for the first time Father Mychal Judge had gone where the temperature was hottest and the stakes highest and emerged with a new understanding of an old problem. It was his way, not to take anything for granted but to seek his own truth. He had been like that since childhood.

Robert Emmet Judge was born in downtown Brooklyn on Dean Street on 11 May 1933, the son of two emigrants from Leitrim, Michael Judge and Mary Fallon, who had met on the boat on the way over to America. The name Michael, which he later took as his religious name (subsequently changing it to Mychal), was likely a tribute to his father, whose grave he frequently visited.

Both his parents grew up on small farms and had little choice but to emigrate. Mary Fallon was one of three sisters who took the emigrant boat to America. When they came over, Michael Judge took a job in Butler's Grocery Store in

Brooklyn. His son was actually a twin; Mychal's sister Dympna was born 50 hours later, a fact she says is borne out by their two birth certificates. He also had a sister, Erin, but a brother, Pearse, died soon after birth.

Times were tough after Mychal's father died from mastoiditis, suffering horribly for three years when Mychal was six years old. The ear infection, easily curable by antibiotics nowadays, spread to his brain and resulted in a slow, lingering death.

Mary Fallon Judge was left in dire financial straits once her husband passed away, though Michael's twin sister Dympna says the family always managed to pull through. Dympna, now living in Berlin, Maryland, where her sister also lives, has very few memories of her father. Her mother, she says, rarely spoke of Ireland but took two trips back to the homestead later in life, which she enjoyed tremendously.

Years later Mychal would bemoan the fact that he, too, never knew his father. "I never called anyone 'Dad'. I've always been very much on my own," he told a Franciscan publication, *The Anthonian*, in 1998.

That early experience of tragedy allowed him a window into the soul of many people who suffered and whom he helped. "When tragedies strike us at an early age, maybe religion takes on a greater meaning. The closer the tragedy is to our heart and home, the more likely faith is to form, because we've been tested and tried and from that comes faith," he maintained.

Despite his young age, Mychal was soon hard at work doing handyman chores around the house. "Although we had nothing my mother always made sure that we felt special," he recalled.

To help make ends meet he often travelled to Manhattan to shine shoes at Pennsylvania Station on the West Side or at Grand Central Station on the East Side. On one of these excursions he stopped in at St Francis of Assisi Church on the West Side and was immediately enthralled by the Franciscan lifestyle.

"I remember the lower church and the fountain and a friar and his brown robe. I used to follow him around everywhere. I had a tremendous urge to be a priest," he said. At age 15 he entered the seminary, and in 1961 he was ordained. He was never happier. Like all Franciscans, he took a vow of poverty and donated all his salary to the order. He even donated his living allowance to the poor, one dollar at a time. Whenever he went out he would take a roll of $1 bills with him. "Being a Franciscan," he said "means never having to write a will."

New York would be his theatre for most of the rest of his life. He loved the city and his native Brooklyn and told *The Anthonian* so. "I love to walk because it releases all the pent-up stuff inside. There is something for me about the Brooklyn Bridge – I must walk across it once a week. I walk from the friary downtown, then across the bridge and maybe keep going to Brighton Beach. I get an ice cream cone there and then come home. I get ideas on the Brooklyn Bridge even when I'm not looking for one. I love to look at the Statue of Liberty, the lights of the city, the Verrazano Bridge, the Manhattan Bridge carrying the subway cars. The city is just the most extraordinary place to live."

He was first posted to St Joseph's in East Rutherford, New Jersey, just spitting distance from Manhattan; then he went to West Milford, also close to the city. There he first came to public attention when he became involved in a tense hostage drama. A distraught man was holding his wife and child at gunpoint in the upper room of his house. When Judge got there he climbed atop a ladder, and police found him gently engaging the man, telling him, "Let's talk it over. We can go and have a cup of coffee. This isn't the way to handle things. Come on down." Shortly after the man came down, handed over his gun and went peacefully with the police.

During his New Jersey years his love of firefighting was evident. "He was a real fire buff, who loved firefighters and their jobs," the Paterson New Jersey fire chief told the *Bergen Record* newspaper.

He served in Rochelle Park in New Jersey and for a period as assistant to the president at Siena College in Loudonville in upstate New York. Then in 1986 came the assignment he coveted, back to St Francis of Assisi Church in Manhattan and, because of his firefighting interest, as a fire chaplain in 1992.

"I always wanted to be a priest or a fireman," he told the *St Anthony Messenger* magazine shortly after he was appointed a fire department chaplain. "Now I'm both. I had to bust my tail to get this habit, so I wear it always. I wanted to be a Franciscan so bad. I have absolutely no regrets."

Father Michael Duffy, a fellow Franciscan and a close friend of Judge who served in New Jersey with him, tells that around this time Judge became famous for his approach to his religion.

"He loved to bless people, whether they wanted it or not, with his big thick Irish hands. He'd put his big hands on, say, a little old lady's head and press down until I thought he was going to break her little neck. He would look up to God with raised eyebrows and pray that God would bless her and keep her in peace. By the end she'd be crying; she'd love it," Duffy remembers.

He had a certain natural bent for compassion, like St Francis, says Duffy. "He just felt bad for people who were not cared for."

Judge treated everyone like family, says Duffy. "Countless people told me that on birthdays, anniversaries, dates of sobriety, whatever – they would get a little note from him. He must have kept a huge calendar. Everyone considered him family."

Soon after moving to Manhattan, Judge became known for ministering to people with the new and then fatal disease of AIDS. Duffy remembers, in particular, one dying AIDS patient who had such a virulent strain that no one would approach him because of the stench.

"Mychal said to me, 'You know no one touches the man. He must feel so lonely.' So he'd go visit him and hold his hand. He told me that once he bent over and kissed him on the forehead because no one would come near him."

Judge never built a church or a school or raised money, Duffy points out. "What he did was build a kingdom spiritually, so people felt close to God. You can't measure that and you can't see that."

Officer Steven McDonald had a cousin, Michael, who died of AIDS. Father Judge was a huge comfort to the family. "Father Mike spent so much time with him, and Patti Ann asked Cardinal O'Connor to go see him, so they did. My cousin went around New York Cornell Hospital bragging about who his visitors were. Father Mychal was there when he died, holding his hand and praying with him. He said my cousin was holding a prayer book he got from the cardinal. It must have been powerful and beautiful."

Soon after moving into Manhattan, Judge became embroiled in major controversy after allowing Dignity, an AIDS service ministry and a refuge for gay and lesbian Catholics, to worship at his church. It was typical of his own need to be inclusive.

"Watching people he was close to being excluded greatly saddened him," says Brendan Fay, co-chair of the Irish gay group, Lavender and Green.

Dignity had been expelled from its home at Francis Xavier Church, and Judge, who as a Franciscan did not report directly to O'Connor, invited them in. The leader of Dignity, Father Bernard Lynch, a native of County Clare in Ireland, who would soon openly proclaim himself to be gay, had become a withering critic of how Cardinal John O'Connor was handling the entire issue of AIDS.

It was a major headache for O'Connor, and it was shaky ground for Judge to be contesting. He never actually celebrated mass for the group but did allow his church to be used for their services and meetings.

Though Judge never publicly "came out", it was evident to many close friends that he himself was also gay. Those closest to him maintain, however, that he remained celibate throughout his life and that his sexual leanings were never an issue.

Officer Steven McDonald is adamant on this point. "There's no one that can demonstrate he ever broke his vows," says McDonald. "I think this whole gay thing shows that some people were not appreciating him for what he was and what he had – a Christlike love for his fellow human being."

Thomas Van Essen, later fire commissioner and a senior Firefighters' Union official in the 1990s, says Judge told him he was gay. "I just thought he was a phenomenal, warm, sincere man, and the fact that he was gay had nothing to do with anything," says Van Essen. Several other friends stated publicly that he was gay, but that it was a matter of orientation rather than practice.

He was fiercely protective of those who he felt were being railroaded because of their sexual preference. Father Lynch had become a focal point for controversy within the church about how they were handling the AIDS issue. He was constantly under fire from conservatives who wanted to be rid of him.

Then in the spring of 1988, Lynch's very freedom was in question when he was indicted on a charge of child abuse on the testimony of a 14-year-old student who swore that the priest had made sexual advances to him at a school in the Bronx. For over a year Lynch endured what he later called "a trial of my very soul". While the charges were progressing, heavy publicity about the case in Ireland meant that his superiors there were reading all sorts of lurid allegations. The silence from the New York archdiocese was deafening, and they refused point-blank to help him in his defence. In his time of need, however, he found a friend.

Convinced that Lynch was being railroaded, Judge flew to Ireland and confronted Lynch's superiors and argued that Lynch was facing a politically motivated prosecution which had no merit. While there he took time out to meet Lynch's father and console him.

As a result of his entreaties, Lynch's superiors agreed to put aside $100,000 for his defence, which allowed Lynch to hire Michael Kennedy, a leading criminal defence attorney. Soon after, the trial completely collapsed, with the judge scathing in his evaluation of the prosecution's case.

Father Judge never forgave Cardinal O'Connor for his inactivity on the Lynch case. Even after O'Connor died, Judge was spotted at his crypt, wagging his finger at it. The idea of abandoning a fellow priest in need would never, ever have crossed his mind.

Lynch, now an AIDS worker in London, acknowledges Mychal Judge's support with deep gratitude. "Mychal's advocacy on that was extraordinary," he told *Lesbian and Gay New York* newspaper. "He had friends in high places and the ear of the cardinal. It was a turning point for me; otherwise I might still be in jail."

Lynch says Judge was an extraordinary man who was "compassionate, complex, brave, hilarious and extraordinary. More than any protest I've known, he took the gospel as a mandate for social justice." Lynch said, "Mychal was unique in that he risked a lot in what he did, and he was extraordinary in his ability to maintain ties with the most sanctimonious of our opponents in the Church."

In addition to his sexuality, Judge also struggled with a drink problem. "He said he didn't know whether it was genetic or what it was," says Malachy McCourt, the Irish actor and best-selling author who went to many AA meetings with Judge. "He said it led him into lunacy. There wasn't much detail about what he did, other than he would find himself in blackouts or in situations he didn't want to be in."

Like everything else that he tried his hand at, Judge soon became a moving spirit behind the organisation. He often led AA meeting himself. He would take a dozen or so members to Long Island for a weekend to help with their recovery.

A huge fan of AA, he once told President Clinton at a White House religious conference that Bill Wilson, the founder of AA and the 12-step programme, was "America's greatest contribution to spirituality" and that he had done more than Mother Teresa to alleviate suffering.

He appeared to have licked the drink problem. In September 2001 he was set to celebrate his twenty-third anniversary of being off the drink. Close friends say that was one of his proudest achievements.

The St Patrick's Day Parade in New York was another controversy Judge dived into. Since 1992 the parade organisers have banned an Irish gay group from walking. The resultant protests and heavy media coverage have dogged the parade ever since. Judge hated the notion of exclusion, and when the Lavender and Green Irish gay group organised a parade in Woodside, Queens, he was supportive. As organiser Brendan Fay remembered in an interview with *Talk* magazine: "We could not get a spiritual leader to open the parade with a prayer. Then on the day of the parade, March 17, 2000, Father Mike, to my deep delight and appreciation, showed up in his Franciscan habit and marched the entire length. He was booed, he got nasty calls and he had to stand up to criticism at chancery levels. To the booers he offered blessings."

In 1993 when the Chinese steamer the *Golden Venture* ran aground off the Rockaway coast, Mike Judge was one of the first priests there and spent days counselling the frightened survivors, all illegal immigrants.

Likewise when TWA Flight 800 crashed into the ocean off Long Island, Judge was a tower of strength for the survivors. There is a famous picture of him from the time, standing on the beach, staring out to sea where the last earthly remains of the victims were. He stayed sixteen days with the relatives of the victims, long days waiting for bodies to be washed up on the beaches around the crash site. He called it one of his toughest undertakings.

"When that call came through, it was the Lord calling me somehow," he told a reporter. "I went out there that night, and I stayed talking to people from all over the country and all over the world."

Father Judge could also display flashes of an Irish temper when he felt someone was being slighted. Officer Steve McDonald remembers that in 1996 he was asked to address the Republican National Convention in San Diego by the chairman of the party, Haley Barbour. Father Mike accompanied him.

"What was in my speech was Northern Ireland, gun violence and the protection of human life," McDonald recalls. "But when the speech came back, everything had been taken out except the part about supporting their candidate, Bob Dole.

"So Father Mike got mad. He grabbed the speech and went down to the organisers. When he came back he said, 'Steven, I just used language I haven't used in 30 years!' By the end of the night they still wouldn't put in the parts about Northern Ireland or gun violence, but I was able to talk about my feelings for human life."

Father Judge was always busy, incredibly busy. Malachy McCourt can testify to that. "There's a very old postcard of a giant Jesus looking in the window of the Empire State Building in these long, long robes – that was Mychal Judge in New York. He was everywhere, all over the city. And how good it was to know he was there. It gave the impression that he had wings under his robes, except you would see him using public transport because he was at everything, helping everybody."

"He was the busiest person alive," says Joe Falco, a fire-fighter from the engine company across the street from Judge's presbytery.

McCourt also believes that Judge had a unique way with people. "He had the extraordinary ability of appearing in a crowd, and it would be as if a light had been turned on," McCourt remembers. "He had that rare quality of making people feel as though they were the only ones in the room. I think the only other person I met with that quality was Bill Clinton."

Father Brian Jordan, a priest at St Francis of Assisi, was enticed into the priesthood by the man who later became his mentor. "I met Father Mychal in September 1996 when I was a junior at Siena College. I wanted to be a lawyer. One day I was walking across campus and I bumped into him. He said, 'What were you doing with the rest of your life?' I said I wanted to be a lawyer. He said, 'Why don't you become a happy priest instead of an unhappy lawyer?' It was a bold thing for someone I hardly knew to say, but I joined the priesthood anyway."

At about 10 o'clock every night, Judge would get home to his simple room in the friary and for the next two or three hours would return the 30 or so messages on his answering machine. Because of the pressure of people trying to see him, Judge had recently had to change the message on his machine, stating that, due to the overwhelming volume of requests, he was unable to do any more weddings or baptisms.

He also kept a journal and would spend hours handwriting thank-you notes or letters of congratulations or consolation to his myriad friends, especially those who were going through a rough spell.

But the fire department had become his first love. No matter what he was doing, he would drop everything to respond to his beeper, which automatically rang if a three-alarm fire was underway.

Often he would go across the street to the firehouse and spend hours with the men, teasing, laughing, telling stories and above all counselling them on problems. He often dropped in to different firehouses around the city on the same work. He had achieved legendary status with the men of the FDNY.

On 10 September he rededicated a firehouse in the Bronx. The ceremony was videotaped by the fire department. "Good days, bad days," Judge says, speaking to a phalanx of firefighters, "but never a boring day on this job. You do what God called you to do. You show up, you put one foot in front of the other, and you do your job, which is a mystery and a surprise. You have no idea when you get in that rig what God is calling you to do. But he needs you – so keep going. Keep supporting each other, be kind to each other. Love each other, work together. You love the job. We all do. What a blessing that is."

On the morning of 11 September, ironically, his beeper never went off. Instead a fellow friar had seen the flames as he walked down Sixth Avenue and alerted Judge. As his friend Father Michael Duffy subsequently said, "He jumped up, took off his habit, got his uniform on, and I have to say this in case you think he's perfect, he did take time to spray and comb his hair" – an allusion to Judge's well-known vanity about his looks.

He rushed to the fire with firefighter Michael Weinberg at the wheel of the fire department car. With the siren wailing they sped downtown toward the World Trade Center.

On his way to the buildings he met the mayor, Rudy Giuliani, who was desperately seeking a new command centre after his old one was destroyed in the attack. As they passed, Giuliani said to him, "Pray for us, Father."

Judge responded, "You know I always do."

What happened next is unclear and has become the stuff of legend, some of it mistaken. It appears that Judge gave absolution and comforted the many dying firemen and civilians whose bodies were already littered on the ground outside the towers. He was not, as mistakenly first reported, hit by falling masonry when he knelt to pray over a dying man hit by a falling body. We know that he then proceeded into the north tower to be with his firemen.

The best clue comes from the extraordinary film by a French television crew, who were filming a documentary on the fire department when the planes hit. In the video, Judge can be seen inside the north tower where the first plane hit, standing with his beloved firemen as all around chaos is breaking out.

Judge is dressed in his firejacket and white helmet. He is off to one side of the firefighters, hands at his side, careful to stay out of their way. His lips move in silent prayer, totally focused on his private communion with his God. Around him police officers, firefighters and emergency personnel from the mayor's office are frantically talking into their cell phones and walkie-talkies. Above him a stream of civilians make their way to the ground floor and safety. Judge is praying furiously, "like Christ in the Garden of Gethsemane", remembers one firefighter.

A man goes over to Judge and shakes his hand. It is Michael Angelini; his father is a member of Rescue 1 fire station and also president of the Firefighters' Catholic Guild. Judge breaks from his reverie and tells the man, "Your mother and father were recently at my jubilee celebration. I will pray for your family, Michael." He pats him in a comforting manner on the shoulder, a typical Mike Judge action.

Then Judge is all alone again, just him and his God. At 9.59 a.m., a huge roar is heard on the tape. The south tower has collapsed. The roar lasts only sixteen seconds, but in that time a massive plume of smoke, pulverised cement and human remains rips through the north tower from the explosion in the other tower, blowing out all the windows and enveloping everything in darkness.

A group of firemen waiting for orders at the tower's emergency centre on the ground floor were caught in the poisonous cloud and dropped to their knees. "Hold hands," someone shouted, and the firemen clung to each other for dear life. Some 20 feet away they had seen Mychal Judge standing just moments before, praying.

As the smoke began to clear, the men reached out and began a slow retreat through the lobby. Lieutenant Bill Cosgrave of the Manhattan traffic task force, of the New York Police Department, who had been near by when the first plane hit, was among them. After about 20 paces, Cosgrave stumbled over a body. One of the firefighters trained his flashlight on the fallen man's face.

"My God, it is Father Mike," he said.

He was relatively unmarked, his body and face completely intact; there was very little debris in the area. It seems Judge died of a heart attack brought on by the enormous stress he suddenly found himself under. His lungs, it was later learned, were full of soot and smoke.

The firemen and Cosgrave placed Judge's body in a neaby chair and carried him out of the building. At that moment, a Reuters photographer, Shannon Stapleton, snapped the photograph that flashed around the world of Father Judge's body being carried out of the wreckage by the firefighters.

Even in death, however, Mychal Judge saved lives. The men who carried him out would very likely have been killed if they had remained inside, as so many of their colleagues were.

When they brought him outside, a medical worker pronounced him dead. Bill Cosgrave screamed for a priest, but there was none present. Instead they decided to bring him to St Peter's, the nearest church. There they placed his body on the altar, his helmet and badge laying on his chest.

The pastor, when he returned, arranged for Judge's body to be brought back to his beloved firehouse, opposite his church. There the firefighters placed their chaplain on a small cot at the back, and they cordoned off the area, creating a makeshift shrine. All the men still standing in the firehouse gathered around his body and to a man began to cry.

Cosgrave and a police officer named José Rodriguez spoke the "Our Father" into the dead man's ear. Mychal Judge had died as he had lived, bravely, without fear, and knowing he was placing himself in the gap of danger.

His funeral was attended by 3,000 people, including every major New York dignitary and former President Bill Clinton and his wife, Senator Hillary Clinton. In his homily, Father Michael Duffy recited the prayer Judge loved to say: "Lord, take me where you want me to go. Let me meet who you want me to meet. Tell me what you want me to say and keep me out of your way."

Duffy, in an inspired eulogy, stated, "Today we bury his body but not his spirit: we bury his hands but not his good works; we bury his heart but not his love."

Father Judge's death certificate listed him as the first documented victim in the World Trade Center. Duffy said that was because there were so many victims who would need help when they got to the gates of heaven, and Father Mike would be there for them, making the introductions. He said he envied Father Judge his death: "He died anointing his fellow firefighters; he died praying; he died talking to God. Then in the flash of an instant he saw the face of God. What a way to die."

"He belonged to everybody, but each person thought he was theirs," said Malachy McCourt in his tribute at a special mass for Judge a month later. "That was the beauty of the man. No one would say a negative thing about him, and I'm saying there must be something, but you know there isn't."

And what would Judge make of his virtual canonisation since his death? McCourt says he would be "howling with laughter, and he'd put a stop to it if he could".

Even the Irish government claimed him as one of their own. Taoiseach Bertie Ahern insisted that Judge be listed among the Irish casualties. It was a nice acknowledgement for the son of Irish immigrants.

For Steven McDonald, the death of Father Mychal Judge was a body blow. It was cushioned a little by the realisation that the man who was probably the closest person to him in the world next to his family had died a hero. "Father Mike is very much alive, and so is his legacy of love," he says.

He reads a letter sent to him from the Reverend John A. Pickering, the pastor of Drumcree church, site of the most explosive stand-off of recent times in Ireland:.

> Dear Steven,
> It was such a great privilege to meet you and Patti and the whole group that day you visited Drumcree Church and to meet Mychal Judge. I'm writing to tell you how sorry I am, along with my parishioners, to learn of the death of Mychal in the New York atrocity, which affects us all, including my wife Olivia, who lost a cousin.

Mychal would have been proud to read that letter, says McDonald, showing we were all brothers and sisters despite our different religions. "That was the message of his life."

CHAPTER NINE

A BIG SISTER REMEMBERS

SEAN PATRICK TALLON, 26, could have been the cool, clean hero of so many American fables. A decorated ex-marine, a beloved former policeman and on the verge of becoming a New York firefighter, the young Bronx man instead lost his life tragically on 11 September when his Ladder 10 Company answered the call of duty. The firehouse was located at Liberty Street, just a half block from the World Trade Center.

They were among the first there. Sean was the irons man, charged with breaking open the doors and gaining access to parts of the building that could not be reached otherwise.

They ascended to the 31st floor of the north tower, where one of the firefighters suddenly had trouble breathing. Sean Patrick Tallon stopped to help him and saved his life by giving him his breathing apparatus. Then he told his stricken fellow fireman that he had to go. There were other lives to be saved, and he disappeared, going onward and upwards, never to be seen again.

The well-known musician Marian Tomas Griffin sang a song she wrote with her husband for the popular young Irishman, whose family hail from County Clare and whose parents had moved back there for a time with Sean and his sister Rosaleen when they were very young.

The last verse ran:

Up the stairs, boys, running to the top
Without a thought of slow or stop.

Up the stairs, boys, on 9-11,
And they kept on going right through the gates of
    heaven.

A few months later, on the IrishTribute.com website,
which remembers those Irish Americans who died on 11 September, his sister Rosaleen wrote a letter to her late brother
that touched the hearts of all those who read it.

"Sean, my earliest memories of you go back to when we
lived in the apartment. We were really little and I remember
us laughing so much with Mom and Dad on the green carpet doing the Twist to Chubby Checker. I remember Dad
shaking you up so fast and you were laughing your head off
and asking to dance over and over again to it. You were
about 2 years old.

"My next memory was when you were 3 years old and
we had moved back to Ireland. It was a winter morning there
and I remember you and I were dressed in matching pajamas
that Dad had brought from his job in Brooklyn. The pajamas
were red, had feet, and giant jelly beans printed all over the
top. I remember us having so much fun on the carpeted stairs
. . . we were getting such a kick out of sitting and sliding
down the stairs. I remember your carrot red hair bopping up
and down as you bounced down the stairs. We were so con-
tented playing with each other.

"My next earliest memory was when we had just
returned from Ireland. You were 4 and I was 7. We shared a
bedroom in our apartment on Rochambeau Ave. Our bedroom faced out to Bainbridge Avenue. At night we would be
scared of the loud sirens of the ambulances and fire trucks
that raced up and down the avenue. (Little did we know that
you would be working aboard both of these trucks later on
in life!) But instead of getting upset to Mom and Dad about
the new noises that scared us, we made a plan that across
our twin beds we would stretch out our arms and hold hands
until we fell asleep. It always worked.

"Sean, I think that throughout our lives we still held
hands through everything and we shared all our hopes and
fears. I will miss that more than I can describe here in words.

"We remember going to so many Irish dancing classes, Irish music classes, and going to all the feises. But the thing Mom and Dad took so serious was our schoolwork. I remember how hard Mom would work with you on your studying. That wasn't always the easiest job either, with your little redhead temper, you could sometimes turn as red as your button-accordion. But they stuck with you . . . I remember Mom and Dad told us that they always wanted us to do as well as we could so that we would not feel bad about ourselves after the test or after the competition or even later in life. And gosh, Sean, you were excited when you would do well . . . and you would always give Dad 'five'. You even gave Dad 'five' when you finished boot camp for the Marines!

"I remember Mom waving out our bedroom window as we walked together to St Brendan's School. We remember when Ms McCarrick, your kindergarten teacher, gave you the big job of saying your little speech . . . you never told anyone until that day . . .

"Through your life, that is how you were. You never made a big deal out of your accomplishments. As a matter of fact, sometimes you were so humble that you made these big accomplishments seem attainable by everyone.

"Humility . . . gosh, Sean, sometimes we were astonished that you would say that others were more capable at just the jobs we saw you do perfectly yourself. For example, you always pushed me out front as the musician and smart one when you had just as much music in you and were sharper than me at a number of things.

"Sean, you wore your insecurities on your sleeve, and weren't ashamed to admit them, whether it was about approaching a girl for a date or being able to pass the physical for the fire department. This amazed me, for such a handsome and fit fellow. But your little anxieties were endearing and made you someone that people could admit their weaknesses to without feeling vulnerable.

"For such a big, strong, tough guy you felt things for yourself and for others very deeply. You made sure that you thought enough about a person's problem so that you could

give some good simple advice. Many of your friends have
mentioned this to me in the last few weeks.

"Another thing that really made you a special person is
that you wanted the best for other people. There are many,
many examples of this. The most recent example was when
your friend Pat was interested in buying the house next door
to Mom and Dad, you made sure that you inquired and
found out that this was a good investment for him.

"As your family, we saw this tough, yet sensitive duality
in you as well. For example, when Rob and I went down to
shake your hand at the sign of peace, you busted his chops
about his, as you said, enormous boutonniere that 'looked
like broccoli' but you told me, 'You look beautiful today.'

"There were so many Christmas cards and birthday
cards . . . it is so great that we saved them because they are
a written reminder of you. In one Christmas card that you
gave to Dad and Mom, it said 'It took me years to realise
that the love you have for me is the closest thing to heaven
that I've ever known.'

"In another you told me not to worry about something,
gave me some tough advice, and then reminded me to take
solace in the fact that my family loved me . . . (in parenthe-
ses you wrote that you weren't sure of the spelling for
solace!! ha ha!!).

"Sean, we all knew that you loved us, and we really
loved you. As your older sister, I always tried to look out for
you and protect you, but sometimes I could not. When you
were little and used to play hide and seek under the bed, you
would bump your head as you scurried out from under the
bed. (It happened more than once.) You would have this big
purple bump on your head and I remember getting so upset
seeing you hurt.

"I remember when you broke your arm in second grade in
the schoolyard and they had to pull on your thumb to straight-
en up the bone and I remember you being in so much pain. I
felt helpless to protect you then, just as I did a few weeks ago.
But I think that God reached down that day to quickly end all
the people's pain at the twin towers. I think he picked you up
into his arms and you are waiting safely there for us.

"I hope that you know how proud I am that you hold the title of US marine. As reservists, you and your fellow marines put in a hard week at work and on the weekends learn how to defend and die for our country. I remember many times when you missed out on weekend events or parties because you had 'duty'. I admire you for joining these men and women and I pray that God will watch over all our military personnel during this time.

"Sean, we will miss your hard-charger intensity and excitement for life. We will miss your strong presence and heavy feet thumping through the house. We will miss you watching the sports with Dad on the couch in the living room while eating a feed of Mom's chicken cutlets. We will miss your car pulling up out front. We will miss you cheering up a tough situation with a witty phrase.

"A funny thing has been happening to me lately, however . . . when I stay quiet for a moment, I feel as if you are whispering a quick, sarcastic phrase in my ear or a quick "just do it" in my ear. I feel your presence, Sean. Your tough, kind presence.

"Mom and Dad have had a hard time calling you a hero . . . I guess that's where you got your humility gene from . . . but they are starting to realise that you are a hero, Sean. We are so sincerely proud of you and that is helping us a little. But it is hard. We pray that you are safe now with God in Heaven.

"We know how much you loved listening to and playing Irish music on the button accordion. We know how much you loved County Clare in Ireland for its great traditional Irish music and the beautiful scenery along the West Coast. We will think of you walking along those cliffs and the sound of the button accordion will be ringing in our ears.

"Sean, I miss you with all my heart. I will try to be as good as I can be so that I can one day laugh again with you in Heaven. Until then I pray that you are happy and at peace with God in Heaven.

"I love you, Sean. I couldn't have asked for a better brother than you. Until we meet again . . .

"– Rosaleen (Sister)"

CHAPTER TEN

ROCKAWAY

ROCKAWAY IS WHERE New York finally gives way to the Atlantic Ocean. The Indian name for this barrier peninsula was "Rechouwacky", meaning "the place of our people". White settlers changed it to Rockaway – a peninsula memorably described in one history book as an "long toeless human foot pointing west".

Situated on the eastern shore of the borough of Queens, it is famous for its sandy beach, which runs the length of the peninsula. Rockaway is a summer haven, an escape from the humidity in the city, but a wild place in winter, first landfall for many of the Atlantic storms that whip up around that time of year.

Off Rockaway Beach, ships from all over the world line up, waiting to steam into New York harbour. The last way station before they reach port, Rockaway lies smack in the middle of one of the busiest sea lanes in the world.

Year round, too, the great jets from all over the world roar overhead, as Rockaway is the landfall closest to the John F. Kennedy International Airport. The constant presence of the planes has become a huge local issue for the residents, who have held major protests in attempts to get the flight paths changed.

The protests took on a more urgent hue when an American Airlines jet, bound for the Dominican Republic, came crashing down at Beach and 120th Street just weeks after the World Trade Center attacks, killing five local residents and plunging a community, already buried in grief, even deeper into mourning.

Hard times have hit Rockaway, but it was not always so. It was once one of the most popular summer vacation destinations in the United States and was famed for its miles-long boardwalk, which still survives, stretching six miles from 9th Street to 126th Street.

From 1850 to about 1950, Rockaway was rivalled only by Saratoga Springs in upstate New York as the summer capital of America. Steamer ferries brought thousands of holidaymakers from Manhattan and Brooklyn, and a rail connection from Jamaica, Queens, brought thousands of other day trippers for a 50-cents round trip. As one historian noted, "Rockaway Beach became an Everyman's paradise."

Nowadays the Rockaway glory days are a fading memory because of far easier access to air travel and a perception that crime and hard times have come to the isolated peninsula. Playland, the great amusement park famous across America, was bulldozed in 1987 because of crime and insurance problems, and with it went the last vestiges of the great summer dreamland.

Many of the social problems originate near the northern shore, known as Far Rockaway, where high-density low-income housing has brought with it a range of concerns not uncommon to any blighted urban area. However, as you move south along Rockaway, the old neighbourhoods still cling tenaciously to their history and culture.

The working-class neighbourhood of Rockaway Beach gives way to Belle Harbor, a middle-class haven, and further down then to the gated community of Breezy Point, where some of the finest houses in all of New York are located. Robert De Niro has a summer home here, as have many of the elite of New York, who find privacy in one of the most exclusive enclaves in the region.

Because Rockaway is cut off from the rest of New York, the neighbourhoods hang together extraordinarily tightly. You have to pass through a toll booth and across a wide bridge to get to the Rockaways, and the only subway line has a very infrequent service.

Though the Manhattan skyline can clearly be seen in the distance, Rockaway is as remote from the great metropolis as a small town in Iowa. "Rockaway marries Rockaway," says Patricia Daly, an advertising executive in Manhattan who grew up in the neighbourhood and married a local guy, as did her sisters.

According to the US census, Rockaway is the second most Irish neighbourhood in America, after the suburbs of Boston. A brief stroll around will confirm that fact. Irish and American flags fly side by side on many homes, Irish-themed bars and restaurants abound, and you can order Irish bacon and sausages from a local butcher's shop specialising in Irish products.

The annual Rockaway Irish festival, held at midsummer, is the rallying point for the tribe, a massive weekend-long affair that usually features bad music, great pints and stands selling every conceivable type of Irish goods from Waterford Crystal down to worthless trinkets.

In Rockaway, being Irish is the norm more than in any other place in New York. Thus, when local political boss James Conway Sullivan died suddenly at age 46 in December 2001, it was no surprise that "Sean South of Garryowen" and "The Wearing of the Green" were the two songs sung at his funeral mass.

The Irish who settled here were primarily from the West of Ireland, and they followed the well-beaten path to job security that generations of Irish before them had followed.

Mick McCarthy from Liscannor, County Clare, came out in 1956 as a lad of 17 on the same day as three other members of his family immigrated. He remembers being steered immediately to Rockaway to an uncle and learning quickly the value a steady job with good permanent prospects held in the community. He joined TWA airlines at the nearby airport and had a long and successful working career there. He met his wife Bridie, from Galway, at a local Irish dance, and they raised their family together on Beach and 109th Street.

Two of his daughters married firemen from the area. Nothing unusual in that. "If you threw a stone in Rockaway, you would surely hit a policeman or fireman," he says. The sons and grandsons of Irish immigrant cops and firemen have followed their fathers in a proud and unbroken tradition of joining the forces. Proportionately, there would be a far higher number of such uniformed men in Rockaway than in any other community in New York.

Thus 11 September hit like a thunderbolt in the Rockaway area. Over 90 men were lost, and for months on end the small community grieved on a daily basis. St Francis de Salles Church, in the heart of the neighbourhood, became a familiar sight on the nation's televisions as funerals and services of those killed in the World Trade Center became everyday occurrences.

Mayor Rudy Giuliani soon came to know his way to the church, and even the hard-bitten mayor, a man whose usual public emotion is anger, broke down at one of the services and talked of the enormous loss of a community.

Thus St Francis became the focal point of much of the grief of the community, and when the American Airlines flight came down only blocks from St Francis, the church quickly slipped into a familiar role of grief and counselling centre.

Father Vincent O'Connell, native of Duagh in Listowel, County Kerry, and a pastor in nearby Breezy Point, tried to explain how the community felt over the tragedy. "It was like the people had no spring, nothing to look forward to," he says. "The scope of the tragedy had blocked their sun."

CHAPTER ELEVEN

MORAN'S MISSION

JOHN MORAN, FROM Rockaway, who was the youngest fire department battalion commander in the department's history, went down in the twin towers blaze. The weekend before he died, John, a talented musician, and his first cousin, Congressman Joe Crowley, had performed at a block party in Rockaway.

"We went through all the old Irish songs: 'The Star of the County Down', 'I'll Tell My Ma,' 'No Nay Never'", remembers Crowley, a rising star in Congress who represents a district in western Queens. Crowley and John Moran were frequent musical partners. On the maternal side, John and Mike traced their roots to the Murphys, from Killeen, County Armagh. In 1998, when Crowley was first elected to Congress, the cousins and a large party went back to South Armagh, the ancestral home, to celebrate. "We sang together every night in the local pubs," remembers Crowley. "Our relatives came from all over to join us. It was a wonderful trip."

One of Crowley's greatest memories is returning as part of the presidential party with Bill Clinton when he visited Northern Ireland in 2000. Though he and the Morans had different political beliefs, it was a proud moment for all the clan to see a relative returning in such important circumstances.

John and Joe remained close throughout their adult lives. The summer before John died, members of the clan, them included, had travelled to Montana for a family reunion. As Joe remembers it, in the Big Sky country the talk was often of Ireland, and the campfires rang with the sound of the guitars of Joe and Cousin John.

On 11 September Joe was sitting on the Washington shuttle from New York, waiting for takeoff and wondering what the delay was on such a perfect day. He called his office, and that was when he learnt the news of the World Trade Center tragedy. Soon after, he remembers, "We rolled back to the gate, and someone on the public address system literally said, 'Go home and be with your families.'" It was a surreal moment.

"I was shocked and numbed," Joe remembers. His immediate concern was for his cousins, firefighters John and Mike Moran. "I was worried more about Mike, John's brother, because John was a batallion commander and Mike wasn't an officer," he said, not knowing that Mike was not on duty. "I guess I felt mistakenly that John would be okay in such a situation. Then I found out it was John who was missing, and as the day went on, it just got tougher and tougher."

Being involved in saving lives and battling blazes was nothing new for the Morans. Their grandfather John Moran came over at age four from Leitrim on 14 April 1903, sailing from Derry along with ten other Moran clan members.

The family were soon involved in the classic Irish professions of tunnelling and the police and fire services. Mike's father and uncle were also instrumental in founding the Sandhogs' Union, for workers who spent their lives in the dangerous profession of tunnelling underground.

There is also a huge tradition of Morans joining the fire department. John and Mike's father and uncle were both members. Another relative, Charlie Moran, was the most decorated fireman in the history of the New York fire department. "They grew up with it all around them," says Crowley.

The outgoing personalities both brothers shared had deep roots, too. John and Mike's father, Walter Moran, was so popular locally that he was known as the mayor of

Rockaway. "He was a larger than life figure," Crowley remembers. "Everyone knew him."

Peggy Murphy Moran and Joe Crowley's mother were sisters, and the clan grew up as an incredibly close extended family. "We were always around each other," remembers Joe. "We spent all our summers out in the Rockaways with our cousins. All of the kids were around the same age."

There was always singing and Irish ballads, and Joe and John were always first up when someone asked for a tune. "We were only waiting to be asked," Crowley says with a laugh.

John was much more than a party person though, according to Joe.

"He was a sensitive guy. He liked history. He was quite brilliant actually; he became a lawyer when still working with the fire department. He could have made a great career elsewhere, but, boy, he loved that department."

John's mother Peggy was also an exceptionally talented woman. "She started off in the lowest rung of a bank and made vice president," Crowley says. "She gave her family inspiration, no matter what they were doing."

In Rockaway, fireman Mike Moran, John's brother, has already become a legend since 11 September. Big and gruff, he is the epitome of the Irish cop or firefighter, and his political opinions definitely reflect the conservative views that many firemen hold.

On this cold December day he has agreed to meet me on the Rockaway boardwalk. He explains that his apartment in a nearby building is "still in a mess" from the aftermath of 11 September because he had been working almost non-stop. When we meet he is dressed in a windcheater and hardly seems to feel the chill wind that comes surfing off the Atlantic.

Mike has been a frequent visitor to his relatives back home and had planned a trip to Dublin in January, but those fellow firemen who were going to come with him were now dead. He is getting married instead, an affirmation for him that life must go on.

Mike Moran became an overnight sensation at the nationally televised memorial concert for all the firemen, featuring

The Who, David Bowie, Mick Jagger, Paul Simon and a plethora of other stars. Also there were leading politicians such as Governor George Pataki, Mayor Rudy Giuliani, former President Bill Clinton and his wife, Senator Hillary Clinton, but it was Mike Moran from Rockaway who stole the show.

He went on stage to tearfully eulogise his brother and the 12 members of his own firehouse. In conclusion, he told Osama bin Laden he could "kiss my royal Irish ass".

People fell off their chairs cheering for Moran. As C.J. Sullivan, a writer for the *New York Press*, wrote, "The best speech given during the 'Concert for the City of New York' was by firefighter Mike Moran. So much else about this concert – for all its good intentions – didn't really give a voice to the cops, firemen, emergency workers and the families of the victims. Celebrities and other dignitaries ruled the stage until Moran seized the moment. And good for him. The firemen went wild."

The *New York Post* reported, "Wild applause shook Madison Square garden when Michael Moran (38) delivered his in-your-face patriotic message to the terror chief, 'Kiss my royal Irish ass.'" As another writer noted, "Moran struck a deep chord with these men who have been under a life and death stress factor after endless days of scouring rubble where the highlight was finding a body part."

Moran himself was amazed by the reaction. "When I said it I had such tremendous tunnel vision I didn't comprehend the reaction. The guys from my firehouse were right there in the front row, and I felt so emotional. The guys were talking later how they couldn't believe the applause, and I asked, 'Did a lot of people applaud?'"

The outburst seemed to capture a moment. Suddenly Mike Moran typified the spirit of the firemen, and he became a national figure himself. Internet chat rooms burned with his name. A band recorded a song called "The Ballad of Mike Moran", to the air of "The Wearing of the Green", a verse of which runs:

Try to take our freedom and you've made a big
    mistake,

The spirit of America you're never going to break.
In remembrance of my brothers, who from earthly
    bonds did pass,
Osama, come on out and kiss my royal Irish ass.

Rush Limbaugh, the conservative talk show host listened to by millions, gave him top billing, as did anchorman Tom Brokaw on the NBC nightly news. In December, Mike Moran was one of a chosen few invited to Westminster Abbey in London for a service to remember the British victims of the blaze, 83 in all.

"I was thinking I'd got over the worst of it, but meeting all those families, 83 from another country, brought it back. I spent a lot of time with a family from Northern Ireland who lost their daughter, who was one of two British people on the second plane that hit the towers. Talking to her family, her mother, sisters, uncles, that brought it all back."

He met former President George Bush Senior, Queen Elizabeth and Prince Charles. It was heady stuff for a boy from the neighbourhood.

John was four years older than Mike and was a batallion chief. He was a member of the elite group known as Special Operations. John was a key figure in helping coordinate all the rescue operations at major fires.

That morning of 11 September, Mike was off duty and John had called him at 7 a.m. to watch a cooking programme which was live on television from Mike's firehouse, Ladder Company 3 on the lower East Side of Manhattan.

After the programme Mike fell back to sleep but was wakened by his girlfriend who told him of the plane hitting the World Trade Center tower. He called his brother, who was speeding towards the scene in the command car with Chief Ray Downey, who was in charge of all rescue operations.

Along the way, other firemen later told Mike they witnessed an amazing incident when a taxi blocked the command car on its way to the fire and John jumped out and manhandled the car off the road. "He was a big guy, about 6 feet 3, 250 pounds," says Mike, smiling at the memory.

Later, during their final phone call, John told Mike he was "right here" at the crash site. Mike speculates that his brother went straight to the second building, which had just been hit when he arrived.

He himself headed immediately for the city. "I went to my firehouse on the lower East Side, and we commandeered a city bus and were just pulling out when we were told to hold ourselves in reserve. World Trade Number 7 was about to collapse, air quality was terrible, no work was possible, and we were told to stay put, try and rest, because they needed fresh men to come on later."

He remembers that he was told that if he wanted to, he could go straight down because his brother was missing. He decided to stay put because, he says, "My brother would want me to act like a professional.

"We went down at 11 o'clock that night . . . the enormity of it all . . . I stood there asking just where do you begin?" Just then, he says, a bunch of Irish construction workers showed up and the leader said, pointing to the outside part of the rubble, "'All right, lads, this is where we start,' and they began working. It was remarkable.

"That first night we were there for 12 hours. When they were holding us in the firehouse, I told my mother, 'It is not good,' because I heard the stories from the firemen who were coming back. After the first night I called her and I said, 'I can't imagine anyone surviving.'" She was very strong, he remembers. "She told me, 'I'm hoping for the best and expecting the worst.'"

The next few days were like a bad dream. "I came home, and I slept a little while. I was exhausted, I was having so many bad dreams I just got up and went back in . . . I felt so bad that he might have been alone. I don't know where he was when he died, but I hope he wasn't alone. It helped when other firemen told me he was probably with a group of civilians. He was the kind of the guy you could turn to at a time like that, like a big brother type."

Mike feels many firemen could possibly have got out. Another captain lost, Pat Browne from Mike's firehouse, radioed shortly before the collapse that they were escorting at least 30–40 severely burned people to safety. As Moran points out, the firemen were all young and physically fit and could easily have saved themselves, "but they insisted on staying to help injured civilians. They could have got out, but they stayed. John was like that."

Since that dreadful day he has taken solace in the vast outpouring of support for the fire department. "People were always pretty nice to firemen. I thought it might be three or four days; it has just built for months. There's a shrine out front of our firehouse. The word went round, for some reason, that firemen in our house needed socks. Well, we got so many socks we almost couldn't get the fire truck in.

"For months all I did was go to wakes and funerals for the guys in the house. It has been very tough. Two a week for 12 weeks . . . so sad when you see all the pain."

He says flatly he doesn't consider himself a hero. "The only act of bravery is when you take the oath and become a fireman. After that it's the line of duty; that's what you expect from each other."

But he also says he is not afraid now in the firehouse when the fire alarm chimes, these days hooked up to a computer, go off. But the memories still haunt him.

"This is extraordinarily hard to deal with," he says, looking out beyond the beach to the ocean. "John had two boys, and I said in his eulogy that their father would never be forgotten. I know that's the case, but it is still very tough. But I do feel he's up there watching over me," he says, his voice breaking.

CHAPTER TWELVE

THE GATES OF HELL

O N THE MORNING of 11 September, Sean Cummins, 38, was sitting at home in Belle Harbor in Rockaway when the two hijacked airplanes smashed into the twin towers.

Cummins, a Dublin-born Squad 1 firefighter stationed in Park Slope, Brooklyn, knew exactly what he had to do – he headed straight for downtown Manhattan to lend his efforts to the incredibly dangerous task of saving lives in the aftermath of the attack.

By the time he made it downtown, both towers had collapsed, and he was still unaware of the horrible news that was lurking around the corner – 12 of the firefighters from his Park Slope station house had been killed when the towers fell.

The roll of honour of the firehouse that day reads: Captain Jim Amato, Lieutenant Ed D'Atri, Lieutenant Mike Esposito, Lieutenant Mike Russo, Firefighter Tom Butler, Firefighter Pete Carroll, Firefighter Brian Bilcher, Firefighter Gary Box, Firefighter Dave Fontana, Firefighter Matt Garvey, Firefighter Rob Cordice, Firefighter Steven Siller. It is near miraculous that Sean Cummins is not among them.

Cummins still has his Squad 1 roster from 11 September. He's on the roster for duty, number 15, along with numbers 12, 13, 14, 16 and 17. That's the way it is in the firehouse. Each firefighter is assigned a number and then the numbers are rostered.

Number 3 (Pete Carroll) was what they call Sean's "24 partner". They shared the 24-hour shift, 12 hours each. That's how they end up doing a 24-hour shift, or "tour".

Sean was owed a tour by Carroll and had called it in because 11 September was the last day of his mother's vacation and he wanted to be able to spend it with her. The deal was that Sean would cover the overnight shift for Carroll and Carroll would come in at 9 a.m. on 11 September for him.

However, there was another complication. Sean, who was due to move to Manhattan's elite Rescue 1 in September, was doing mandatory scuba training for Rescue 1, and the training session had been changed from 18 September to 10 September. Carroll, however, told him that another firefighter, Steve Siller, owed him a tour, so Sean would be covered.

It was Marie Cummins' first visit to America in two years. She was coming to see grandchildren, Sean, 7, and the twins Hannah and Tara, 5, before they became strangers.

She had originally been due to arrive on 1 September and leave on 11 September. However, it turned out that the first was sold out and the earliest available date to come out was 5 September. She decided to take it and return on 11 September as originally planned, despite an offer of extending her trip to the 15th. Sean and his mother were going to hang out, perhaps do some shopping, and then Sean was going to drive Marie from his Rockaway home to JFK for the 6.50 p.m. Aer Lingus flight to Dublin.

Sean was born in Dublin, and his father John was a well-known boxer. When Sean was young the family moved from Finglas in Dublin to a place near Tara in Meath where they raised horses. Sean and his three brothers, Michael, Neil and Robert, loved to box, and their father also encouraged them to ride horses.

"He never pushed any of us to go into boxing, but I think he would have liked it. I don't think he ever got over the fact that I was good at the triple jump, of all things.

"When I was 17, I qualified for the county finals and then qualified for the All-Ireland. Coming home from the county qualifiers, my father turned round and said, 'Whoever heard of the triple jump?' That was the end of that. I didn't compete in the All-Ireland and I never did the triple jump again."

Sean says he wasn't much of a student. "When I passed my inter, I don't know who was more surprised, me or the people I knew!"

Instead of staying in school he went to the government-run training agency AnCO, where he started learning construction. "I was doing a lot of horse racing then; it was great, being so young and earning money for what was a lot of fun for me."

Sean's first trip to New York was in 1983 when he came over to visit his brother Michael, who was living here at the time.

"I hung out for a month during the summer, and when I came back in 1985 I met Maureen in a pub called the Beanpost on Fifth and 76th Street." Maureen was from Brooklyn, so they had a transatlantic romance for a couple of years before eventually marrying in 1989.

He went straight to the navy recruiting office from the INS office once he got his papers in 1990. Three years later, he received his citizenship on the accelerated citizenship path reserved for those who have signed up. Sean says he's always loved the uniformed services. Maybe it was growing up in a family full of brothers.

"At one point I wanted to be a paratrooper, but I was Irish and the only option in Ireland was the British army. Which wouldn't have been the thing to do. I even thought of joining the foreign legion or the Australian army, but instead I ended up in America."

He spent three years in the navy, during which time he took the FDNY test, and five years in the army. He joined the FDNY in February 1996 – with two years of his army service left – and even then he was attending airborne school at the age of 33. "I was the second oldest guy in the class.

"One of the first guys I met in the FDNY was Gerry Dewan. We went through proby [probationary] school together. He and I really hit it off. Both of us were, like, out-of-towners. He came from Boston because he couldn't get into the fire department there, and we just got on really well.

He moved into our house two years ago and rented our basement. It was great; it was like having a brother in the house.

"All of my family are in Ireland except for Neil, he's in
England, and I missed that friendship. I depended on Gerry
more than I realised. I'd say, 'I'm going down to see Gerry,'
and I'd be gone for two hours, just doing guy stuff. He was
great with the kids, too, and when he was here and I was at
the firehouse, he'd always check to see if Maureen would
need anything. He'd let a roar: 'Mo, need anything in the
shops?' and off he'd go for the messages, especially in the
winter.

"He really was like a brother to me. I'd even yell at him
for doing something stupid. He would be the guy who I'd be
talking to right now. Maureen called him our fifth child, me
being the fourth."

Maureen adds: "We're just trying to clear Gerry's apartment out. He was our friend. His family have become our
friends, too. It's just so final. He's gone, yet his apartment
looks as if he's still living here, and his car's still in the
driveway."

Sean and Gerry were both sent to Engine 217 in Brooklyn. By January 2000 Sean was in Squad 1 in Brooklyn while
Gerry worked in Manhattan. "It's a very close-knit world in
the firehouse. You're either in or you're out, unless you're a
wife, and even the wives don't know what it's like. There's
also that long tradition of 'Don't bring the fire home.'

"Single guys like to work the holidays. It's like a family
to them. Instead of being on their own, they're with the guys.
People get on better in the firehouse than they do with their
own family. Some of the guys used to joke that this was an
easier house than their own one. You're there for 24 hours,
so you do get very close.

"They say the difference between the boy scouts and the
fire department is that the boy scouts have adult supervision.
And it's an oxymoron when you say you want to be a fireman when you grow up. You can't – it's either one or the
other.

"I discovered in the fire department that two guys might
hate each other, but in a fire you know you can depend on

each other. There's no crap over race, colour, whatever. You're a fireman and that's it.

"I used to always get in early and work out, go downstairs at 8 o'clock and be sitting in the kitchen breaking everyone's chops. One of the great things is that even if you screw up it doesn't matter, 'cos come a couple of hours later, someone else will have screwed up and you'll be off the hook.

"I still hang out with some of the guys from the firehouse, but it's not the same. My buddies were the guys I worked the shifts with.

"Tommy Butler, he was a great guy. Tommy and I used to talk about becoming fire marshals, which is like a detective except you investigate arson. I used to say that he'd have to be the bad cop and I'd have to be the good cop because he's so miserable.

"That was the big joke in our firehouse: 'When are these two going to become fire marshals?' We were going to take the next test when it came up, and it became a running joke: what kind of a car would we drive? You know, all that kind of stuff.

"Every day at 5 p.m. we'd sit down to watch *Magnum*. We even called Tommy 'Tommy Butler Magnum'.

"Me and Tommy were also going to take classes in Arabic . . . but that ain't gonna happen now.

"Now Tommy's gone and it's hard. Sometimes it really, really hurts. It just hurts. You can actually feel how much it hurts.

"I have a video of all of us camping up together: me, Tommy, Gary, Matt, Jimmy Lopez, Paul Stallone and Joe O'Donell. Myself and Gary went up together. We went camping and white water rafting up in Pennsylvania in May. It was brilliant. Just the lads.

"I watch the video sometimes to remind myself what they were like. In case I forget. But I'll never forget them. We ate, slept and drank in the firehouse, and like the camping trips, sometimes we'd just go off on trips together.

"Ordinarily, most firehouses do something like that. I don't know if anyone's doing it now. I try and hang out with the guys, but it's not the same. All my friends died in the towers."

His wife Maureen says that sometimes she thinks Sean wishes he had been in the towers, too. That he hadn't been off-shift that day.

On the day, Maureen had left the house to drop the kids to school when Sean and his mother saw what was happening at the Trade Center. "We switched on the TV and the first thing I did was call my brother Robert in Ireland to tell him I was okay.

"I knew I would be called in, but I needed to wait for Maureen to come home so she could stay with my mother. I knew this was going to be a big job, and I didn't know when I would be able to contact her again. We didn't have any cell phones before 11 September."

However, Maureen was delayed coming back from the school as she had walked the two blocks to the bay, to see what was happening in lower Manhattan. "We could see the smoke from Rockaway because, you know, it was so clear that morning," says Maureen.

Maureen's detour added another few minutes on to her trip home, and as she came in through the front door at 9.28 a.m., the phone was ringing. The FDNY was ordering a complete recall of its 11,228 firefighters for the first time since the blizzard of 1947. Sean grabbed what gear he had in the house, said his goodbyes to his wife and his mother, and made his way to the firehouse.

"By the time I got down to the firehouse, I was in the middle of a bunch of guys who were getting ready to go in." The only person who had left was Eddie D'Atri. He signed out of the firehouse to say he was going to the Trade Center.

"We have a journal, and Eddie wrote in at 9.40 a.m., and we know that Eddie was in the north tower. I spoke to a guy who saw Eddie racing up the stairs of the north tower after we saw the south tower coming down. These guys knew the north tower was coming down, and they knew they weren't fighting the fire. They went in there to get the people out.

"Most of the guys had already left, so we started loading up an SUV with what we had – which wasn't much.

Everything was on the rig. Billy Reddan, Jimmy Lopez, Joe Mlynarczyk, Paul Stallone and myself were ready to head in when an FDNY communications truck pulled up and offered us a lift. We'd more room in the truck, so we put on some baskets for carrying people, Stokes baskets, and we headed down Flatbush Avenue, on the wrong side of the street."

A police car saw what they were trying to do and moved up to lead the mini-convoy over the bridge and into lower Manhattan.

"By the time we crossed the bridge, the buildings had already collapsed. The Brooklyn Bridge was shut down after we crossed it."

Sean and his little company from Squad 1 crossed into mayhem. Sean heard that other firemen hid in ambulances to cross the bridge. They passed thousands of people fleeing lower Manhattan.

When they got to the towers they were shocked by what they saw. "It was an unbelievable sight. It was so over-whelming that my brain just could not take it in. There was this thick dust everywhere, and it made everything look the same. It was hard to make out any shapes in the haze.

"There were no people there. I thought I would see loads of people there. We all thought that there would be people everywhere, that we would be doing medical work, getting people into the ambulances. But there were no casualties there. Then I saw four guys from my old company, 217, come staggering out. They had got caught in the collapse and they were missing two guys.

"We were looking for stuff from the rigs that were left there, and we met this guy who was trying to get us to go in and put this fire out. He kept saying: 'C'mon, we can put this fire out. C'mon, we can put this fire out.' But the whole frig-ging world was on fire. Two of the big guys got him and escorted him out because we couldn't leave him there.

"We'd started working our way around this enormous mess, and we came across this shoe, one single shoe. It was the first personal belonging I had seen. Then we saw some-one from 5 Engine Company. He said he was missing some-one. 'We're missing one guy, we're missing Manny.'

"At this stage everyone would have been missing. But we didn't know. I mean we sort of suspected, but we didn't know, you know? We were thinking the best.

"We split into groups and started searching the streets; and as we went past Building 5, we heard someone shouting, 'We've found someone down here.'

"We went through Building 5, underneath the plaza, towards the voice, and we could see this figure perched on top of the rubble where the plaza used to be. To this day still I don't know where he came from – he could have been in the plaza when the buildings collapsed – but he looked as if he had come straight from the top of Building 5.

"People were telling us that there was a hose line near by, so Joe starts making his way over to the guy while we go looking for the hose line to put the fires out so we can rescue him.

"But we can't find this hose line, and everything is still screeching, twisting and turning round us. The stores were wrecked, the train is stopped right underneath us, and we can't find this hose line. So, we have to go back to this guy and try and rescue him without being able to put the fires out, and they're moving closer all the time.

"It's dark down there, and we're using civilian flashlights that we had taken out of the stores. We had none of our own gear, no masks, no flashlights, nothing, because everything we had was on the rig.

"We eventually came back out without finding the hose line, and the chief is ordering everybody out [of Building 5] because there's gas there, so all the guys were going out, but we can't see Joe Mlynarczyk.

"There's no way we're going out without Joe, and we know he won't leave the guy stuck there. So we ran past the chief, and he knew he wouldn't be able to stop us – our type of squad wears a gold insignia, and he would have known there was no point trying to stop our kind of squad. He knew he would have been wasting his time if he had tried to. It would have been, like, 'Okay, Chief, goodbye.'

"That was a decision that we took, to try and save this guy. That's what we're paid for, and if you don't want to do it, then you should leave the fire department. So we're going in as these guys were coming out. Some guy shouted at us, 'He's in there, he's in there.' So we go in and there's ammonia gas spreading all over the place.

"Then we hear Joe guiding us to him, 'I'm in here, I'm in here.' So we crawl up over the rubble, and we find him with this guy, who's got to weigh somewhere between 250–300 pounds. The guy's trapped underneath steel and his legs were caught.

"I remember thinking, 'This is bad, this is real bad.' We were being sprayed by the ammonia and the fires were coming nearer and nearer. Everything was falling in on us, the fires were getting closer to us, we're getting sprayed with this inflammable gas, and I'm, like, 'I guess we're done right here.'

"I was the most scared I have ever been in my entire life. Completely scared. I was thinking I was sure I was going to to die, right there. I was thinking, 'This is how it's going to happen.'

"So, we just went to work. What else could we do? We strapped up this guy. We put him in webbing that we had carried across. He was conscious and moaning, and I suppose fear and frustration drove me to say stuff I wouldn't normally say: 'You've got to help us move you; if you're not going to help us, you're going to fucking die!'

"So he tried to roll over, and at this stage another guy, from, I believe, Truck 119, had come to help us, and after about ten minutes, when other firefighters realised we were still there, they sent in a Stokes basket and we were able to drag him back to the street.

"We got him to an ambulance and we sent him on his way."

After rescuing the unknown man (Sean doesn't know if he survived, or even what his name was), the firefighters reassembled outside Building 5, which was still ablaze.

"It was completely gutted, with flames shooting out of the top. We could see firemen on the top, and initially we thought they were trapped. Thankfully they weren't.

"It took us an age to get to the Millennium, where we planned to regroup. [In ordinary times, the Millennium

Hotel was a short walk across the street from Building 5.] At
the Millennium we hooked up with some more guys who we
knew, and we searched the [ground] floor of the hotel. We
found a motorcycle in there, and the phones were working.
It was so weird. A motorcyle? Where did that come from?
Plus the phones working, that was really strange. Soon, there
was a beeline of people going straight to the phones.

"We decided to try and work our way around this mess
and work our way down to where we believed our guys
were. We're going around the pile, trying to work our way
to the other side of the pile, to the west side of the twin
towers. You couldn't go through the middle. There was no
middle.

"So we'd started to work our way around when one of
the guys said: 'You do realise that we're going to have to get
back to the firehouse? The phones are going to be ringing off
the hook. The wives are going to be calling.'

"At this stage, that hadn't dawned on us. That was
going to be a thankless job, that wasn't going to be a job I
wanted to be doing. I could imagine what the wives must
have been going through. No information, no one knew
anything. We didn't know anything, and we were right
there. Anyway, three of the guys were sent back to start
answering the phones, and the rest of us stayed there, trying
to find our rig."

They made their way south from the Millennium to try
to get across to West Street.

"It wasn't easy getting round, but we just kept going,
working our way round, working our way round, and that's
where we came across our first dead person. It was a woman
with a wedding ring on; it seems that everyone we came
across that day had a wedding ring on. Someone had already
covered her with a sheet. Because we were in triage mode,
we were searching for casualties and remembered where the
dead ones were.

"And it wasn't easy getting round. We'd keep working
our way round, working our way round, but it was so pre-
carious. Some of the drops were upwards of 40 feet and
we've all this gear on us.

*Ruth and Juliana McCourt who died aboard United flight 175
when it crashed into the World Trade Center.*

Father Mychal Judge with Police Officer Steven MacDonald and his son Conor who accompanied him to Ireland.
Photo: Nicola McClean/*Irish Voice*

*Donna and Mike Moran. Firefighter Moran became a hero to mil-
lions of Americans when he blasted Osama bin Laden during a
memorial concert.*
Photo: Nicola McClean/*Irish America*

Marian and Bruce Reynolds on their wedding day. He was a frequent visitor to his wife's home place in Donegal and gave his life saving others.

Sean Cummins, a lucky survivor; his mother changed her return flight to Ireland, which saved his life.

In Loving Memory
of

Moira Ann Smith

Memorial Mass
THURSDAY, FEBRUARY 14, 2002 — 2:00 p.m.

CATHEDRAL OF SAINT PATRICK
New York, New York

Police Officer Moira Smith died saving others and left a two-year-old daughter behind.

Damian and Joann Meehan with son Damian Junior. Damian almost made it out on 11 September. His daughter, Madison, was born a few months later.

Liz Smith, who lost her boyfriend, Mike Andrews, on 11 September.
Every day she could see the Twin Towers on her way to work.

Denis Kelleher, a Kerry native who was stranded in Canada in the aftermath of 11 September. His Wall Street office narrowly escaped the impact.

"Eventually we found both of our fire trucks on West Street. One of them was completely crushed. The other one was partially crushed."

They knew it was their truck because Squad 1's trucks had certain things added to them. "It wasn't a regular engine; it had a box on top for the hazardous materials. You would spot the special steel box a mile away. You would know your own truck, and ours was just that little bit different."

Someone had brushed away the debris to reveal the insignia – and someone had written their colleagues' names in the dust covering the truck: "*Lt Espo, – bro. Fontana, Garvey, Siller, O'Donnell. We love you guys.*"

Joe O'Donnell was actually alive. He was wrongly thought to have been in the first call-out. "We didn't know who had been called to the towers, so we could only guess that they were all gone.

"I tried getting in the rig to get what we call our riding list. It lists all the people on a call-out, and it's duplicated, one for the officer and one to stay in the truck in case no one comes back. Normally the truck doesn't get crushed. But the rig was completely crushed, and we couldn't get in to get that out. It was the first time we had thought that maybe we wouldn't be finding any of Squad 1.

"Between 3 p.m. and 4 p.m. was a kind of downtime, waiting to find out when we were going to go into Building 7, which was still blazing. One of the guys has a cell phone and it's working, so I call Maureen to tell her we're okay and that we're going into Building 7 to put the fire out."

For Maureen Cummins, who knew her husband had missed the initial collapses, her day was about to pitch into stomach-clenching fear.

"I'm watching the TV with my mother-in-law all day, praying that Sean's all right, the squad's all right, when I get this phone call. Sean says he's doing fine and they might be going into Building 7 to put the fires out. So we carry on watching the TV when suddenly they break the coverage with a newsflash: 'Building 7 Collapses! Building 7 Collapses!'

"I thought he was gone. I'm screaming, 'He's gone, he's gone!' My mother-in-law starts crying. And we're hysterical.

It was the worst time of my life. I really thought he was
gone."

Ten minutes later, the newscaster comes back with an
updated report. "No, that was a scheduled collapse," says
the announcer. "I'm sorry for the earlier report. That was a
scheduled collapse."

Her husband says he had no idea what was happening in
the outside world. "We had no idea what the TV was reporting. We had been supposed to put the fire out, but then we
found out we had no water. The mains had been crushed and
there was no water pressure. It went against everything we
do, but we got out of the building. We were going to let the
building collapse. We're completely screwed. We want to
fight this fire but we've no water. It's free burning.

"The chief said, 'We really want to fight this fire, but I'm
not risking any more people.' It was a great move by the
chief. But Maureen doesn't know what I know, because I'm
standing right there when it collapses and I know it's been
evacuated."

Meanwhile his wife and mother were still frantic with
fear. "Me and my mother-in-law just stayed by the phone. I
wasn't leaving the house unless I knew where he was, and he
knew where I was. Especially after the Building 7 scare,"
says Maureen. "We stayed in all the first day. They rang the
church bells that night for anyone who wanted to go and
pray, and my mother-in-law went, but I wouldn't go."

Back on the pile Sean Cummins was still looking for
people to save. "After Building 7 collapsed, we went through
Number 2 World Financial Center and got right out on to
the pile. We can hear what we call a pass alarm. If a fireman
is motionless for more than 30 seconds, this pass alarm starts
beeping. And we hear these pass alarms going off.

"There's just three of us now, Paul Stallone, Jimmy Lopez
and myself, and we head out on to the pile. The pile is empty.
It's just the eeriest thing. Complete and total silence, just one
or two other people out there and these pass alarms.

"The northern overpass is partially collapsed, so we went
under there and saw Rescue 1's truck, which was partially
crushed, and 3 Truck. That's where we found the entrance

into the PATH train. The PATH train at that point was completely dry, and we're working away along the tracks, and we can hear stuff moving above us and this awful grinding noise. We decided to drop down underneath the PATH train and try and search the pile. We thought we could make our way underneath the rubble and then dig our way up.

"Everything is moving up top, and we can hear this grinding underneath and above us, and then this lieutenant comes along and tells us to get the hell out. No one knew if the street levels would hold. He was ordering everybody out, and the pity of it is that when they did try to get in three days later, it had flooded.

"We dug and moved and dug for hours and hours, and we ended up digging round the fire trucks out on West Street where people would have tried to take cover. The first person we found looked as if he had been walking on the street when he was killed. He was trapped underneath steel, and when we pulled him out we found a wallet and a wedding ring on him.

"Some ironworkers saw us and called us over, pointing up to the pile. And there's a woman up there, completely naked; her clothes have been blown off her. She looked as if someone had placed her there gently. She looked as if someone had just placed her hanging over this piece of steel.

"Then we saw this other woman's hand pointing up towards the sky. It looked wrong. The woman's hand was perfectly manicured, and, of course, she had a wedding ring on. And then we realised we could see lots of hands. But we couldn't move them, we couldn't put people in body bags straightaway as there was too much stuff lying on top of them, around them, and there was nothing we could do for them. You could find someone, but you couldn't remove them because it was like a big Meccano set. You had to move hundreds of tons of stuff to get to one person."

Later that evening the pressure began to tell on the firefighters. "Billy Reddan and I took some aspirin and candy and sodas from the nearby stores, looking for batteries for flashlights. We all had headaches. We decided to split the group up, and some guys went home. I volunteered to stay on.

"I remember a building still burning near the south tower, and there was nothing we could do about it. We felt so useless. We're supposed to be firemen and we could do nothing about it."

Cummins stayed at it all night until dawn broke the following day. "You know how people talk about the grey light of dawn. It was the worst dawn I've ever seen. It was, like, 'Holy shit – what happened here?' We were slumped beside two ambulances, and as dawn broke you could really see the violence.

"As the sun came up we could see these two feet sticking out from behind an ambulance. It was only about 50 feet away. This guy must have taken cover behind the ambulance when the towers started to collapse, and the ambulance must have crushed him.

"We headed back to the firehouse later that day, and the phones were ringing off the hook.

"We changed and we were getting ready to go back in again, and somebody said this is not a short-term thing. We better eat, get some rest, so I went home, and when I got there people had already started arriving with food for the firehouse.

"When I went back, one of the retired captains came by and told us to go upstairs and lie down, just go lie down, and he took care of all the calls. That was one of the great things, you know. Retired firemen just came straight back to their old firehouses to lend a hand.

"The first of our guys that we found was Petey Carroll, my 24 partner and the guy who had picked up my shift. He was found on the Wednesday night [12 September].

"I was there when we found Captain Amato towards the end of September. He was wearing one of our lieutenants' coats, so we thought it was Lieutenant D'Atri. We weren't sure who we had found first. We couldn't tell who he was. We couldn't even identify our own captain at this point.

"I tell people that nobody there suffered. We don't describe how people were found, because people really don't need to know. The best way I've heard it described is that when the building came down, it was like a giant blender.

That's what it did to people, but they would have been already dead. I can honestly say that no one I saw suffered; they died instantly. Not one of the people I found would have been lying there conscious, not even for a minute. And we saw a lot of people, we dug out a lot of people. One guy I found, my arm went straight through him, right up to my elbow.

"My biggest fear later on, when we were checking the holes, the voids, was that we would find someone who had lain there waiting for rescue. You're hoping to find people, but your biggest fear *is* finding people. I had nightmares about finding people lying up against walls, jackets off, waiting for you to come. But it did not happen. We went into so many holes, and none of the guys found anyone like that. We found so few bodies there: we were carrying hands and feet most of the time. We heard a million rumours about people being found like that, and it didn't happen, it just did not happen.

"The amazing thing is, you drop two levels below the plaza and there's cars there completely intact, the alarm light flashing, letting you know the car's fine, in the midst of this terrible destruction. You could see kids' toys, like I saw a little cuddly toy completely in one piece, right beside a piece of steel that was completely mangled. No sense to it.

"There wasn't a piece of glass to be found, yet this building had been nearly all glass. Where was it? Later on they told us, what we were breathing was crushed glass, crushed concrete and people.

"It's going to break people's hearts when they finally lift the last stone out of there – and everybody isn't found. It's going to hurt so many people. It's going to be rough; it's going to be tough to deal with. People are just naturally assuming that everyone will eventually be found.

"Nobody knew the south tower was going to collapse. All the firemen would have been trying to evacuate people, making sure everybody was out. They would have known that there's no fighting this fire. They would have been spread out all over the offices, as high up as they could go.

"The reason they found so many people in the north

tower was because so many were in the stairwells. They pro-
tected people from being completely crushed. The ironworkers would lift up the layer of steel covering the stairwell,
and we'd come along and search, and that's where we found
so many people.

"Our friend Gerry's watch was still working when he
was found. His Claddagh ring was perfect. How could they
survive when the world fell down on him?

"There's so many ifs and buts: why they were working;
why wasn't I? There's no rhyme or reason to it. You wonder
then, am I here for a reason? Why am I here and my friends
aren't? Why was the scuba class rescheduled? Why was
Maureen dropping the kids to school? Why didn't my mother change her dates like the travel agent expected her to?

"It's the weirdest thing to see my number there for the
11 September shift and knowing that every other number
down to work with me died. You see, all those guys around
me, all the guys I worked with were gone. Plus another six
from my squad.

"We're the type of guys who were going to go into the
towers. That goes for all firemen. You're not going to stop
us, that's why we're in these companies. We want to go to
stuff like this. We don't want to die or anything. We like
going to fires. We like doing that kind of stuff.

"And in the end it's got nothing to do with anything. It's
nothing to do with how good a fireman you were. I consider some of the guys who got caught in there great firemen.
Incredible firemen. But when a building falls on you, it has
nothing to do with your ability. It didn't matter who you
were on 11 September. Unless you could sprout wings and
get out of that building, you were done for.

"For 6 Truck to survive is really a miracle. I was in that
stairwell in the tower, where they were found. If they had
been one flight up or one flight down, they all died. That was
winning the Lotto. That was a miracle. They didn't even
know the towers had collapsed. It's absolutely amazing that
they lived. It blows my mind. I've been up and down that
tower, or what's left of it, and it is incredible that they
weren't sucked down with it. All bets were off that day.

"I think my dealing with it was put off. Other guys dealt with it up front, and maybe they were better off. I think I'm probably doing worse now, four months later, than I have been doing the whole time. I'm missing the guys. I'm really missing the guys. It's only hitting me now.

"I don't sleep in the bunk room any more. I go straight to the top floor. I never ever used to do that before. I used to go in early in the mornings to the firehouse, just to beat the traffic, work out, shower, shave.

"Normally I'd be downstairs at 8 a.m., 'Does anybody want to go? Let somebody else go.' And I don't do that any more. If somebody asked me I would gladly do it, but I don't volunteer it.

"I love the fire department. I'll never leave it, but it can be a very cruel place if you've a thin skin. They'll eat you alive, those boys. If you flinch at anything, you've had it.

"I heard about this one guy who was down at a fire, and he told the chief, 'I'm just going outside for some air.' And that was it, he walked away. Everyone on the job was getting really worried because they didn't know where he was; and then someone went to his house, and he'd barricaded himself in. They had to take him away."

Maureen hosts a counselling group for wives of surviving firefighters every week in the kitchen of her home.

"Our group got started after I was talking to this woman one day at the pool. I felt like everything was getting on top of me. I was snapping at the children, and I don't usually, and I was getting really worried when Sean was out of the house. Just him being gone would make me very anxious. Sean was gone for 24 hours out of every 72, and his spare time was spent at the neverending funerals and memorials which took place from 12 September.

"I was talking to this other wife and telling her how I was feeling, and she said she felt the same, too. It was great to find someone else who had the same panic and fear I had. We both thought that we were going crazy. And we knew that we had to do something.

"I rang the Catholic Charities, and I went there myself first and asked them could they come see us as a group, because I knew there were other wives of surviving fire-fighters who felt the same way and we needed to talk.

"The counsellors told me that it was finally catching up with me, and that maybe it was only hitting me now that I could have lost him. They talked about how much he meant to me and that maybe I hadn't thought about that for a long time.

"I don't know what I would do without him. I don't know how all these other wives [of victims] are coping. I feel so bad for them. It's indescribable what they must be going through. I mean, they have to stay strong for the kids. How do they do it?

"We've both bought cell phones since 11 September, and we're on the phone four or five times a day. And I'm also worried that I'm calling the firehouse too much, but it doesn't matter because everyone understands. That's why we have the cell phones now. I never thought in a million years that I would break down and get a cell phone."

Sean has also started to stay in touch much more. "I've told Sean Jr and the girls that if they ever need to talk to me, just call me on the cell phone. Because they worry. They worry when I go off to work, because they know other people's daddies didn't come home. And now they worry about flying. They were scared when I flew to Ireland.

"And they know Gerry's gone. Gerry's apartment down-stairs has been cleaned out just this past weekend.

"I wasn't here so much that we were getting really worried about the kids. So we went to a counsellor after one of the funerals, Mike Russo's funeral. He called us in individually, spoke to me, called Maureen in, and he told us: 'I don't need to speak to the kids. It's you I need to speak to,' meaning me.

"'What they need is you home,' he says. 'You're alive, but if you're not there you're just as missing as the other fathers.' In their minds, you're not here, so does it really matter if you're alive or dead? You're not there, you're missing; you're the same missing as anyone."

Maureen also worries about the mindset of the firemen and how they are handling the awful events. "The first day we had the group, this girl said, 'They should have been debriefed,' referring to the guys; and the first day of our session, it was all about the guys. The chaplain didn't have to say anything, it was all about the guys. And out of our group, none of our husbands have gone yet to get help. It's almost as if we're helping them by proxy.

"I can't count the amount of times I've tried tricking him. He's telling me stuff, and I'm trying to get him to tell the counselling unit. And they do need help, but this macho thing is holding them back, and even if they did it as a group it might come out. And then they'd realise like me and that girl at the pool that day, 'It's not just me feeling like this. I'm not alone in this.' And it would help them feel better."

Sean points out, "But we've had guys gone to counselling."

Maureen, however, says, "But then you all make fun of him and call him crazy."

Sean seems to make her point. "Ah, no, that's a joke; but yeah, he is crazy."

Sean is moving to Rescue 1 soon, and Maureen wants him to call all of the wives of the firemen who died from Squad 1, to let them know he's going.

"He needs to call the wives of the husbands who he was close to. Even though they knew he was due to leave in September, it's still better for him to call and tell them rather than for them to walk into the firehouse one day and find him gone."

Sean has come to agree with her. "It took me a while, but I'm coming round to that way of thinking now.

"A lot of the things I am dealing with now, I may be judging people by my standards, which Maureen says I am wrong to do, and she's probably right. I have a set way of doing things, be it right or wrong, but it's my way of doing things. I don't know whether it's right, but I try to deal with it in my own way. I like going down to the pile to dig. There's only, I think, three of us left who don't mind doing it. I want to go down there, dig right down for the guys.

"I have no problem digging the guys out. I have more of a problem, at least I did earlier on, dealing with the widows.

And the widows said it: 'No one can look us in the face.' And I guess that's human nature.

"My mother had told me that after my father died that she would meet people and they wouldn't mention him. And that's not what she wanted. She wanted to talk about him. So any time I talk to the widows, I'll talk about something I did with them. I called up Denise Esposito and we were talking about what me and Espo would be doing in the firehouse and stuff, and she goes: 'You're my hero. You've made me laugh today.' And this was late in the afternoon.

"And it did make me feel good. I said to her that my mother had told me, 'Do talk about it. Don't not talk about it.' And she said she felt better, and I know that I felt better.

"Leaving the firehouse now is tough. But things will work out. We'll come back from it. Some people will become stronger, some people won't.

"I think a lot of people are going to leave the fire department. A lot of guys feel obligated to stay until the site at Ground Zero is finished, and I've even heard some guys without time saying that they're leaving. They're so upset and hurt at losing so many people, so many friends.

"One guy I know worked on boats, he came from a salary of about $100,000 to the firehouse, where he was making about $30,000, but he moved because he loved the job. He's leaving now, and who can blame him? He's lost so many friends that he just doesn't want to stay around and be reminded of it.

"It's going to be rough all the way round. I don't think we've seen the half of it yet. I think there's going to be waves of suicide, broken marriages, guys going off the rails. Now it feels like catch-up time for me. It feels like the worst time.

"The fire department is the real macho image. You don't cry, whatever. I was a paratrooper, a commando. It's fine. Suck it up, deal with it.

"I think I've been really good. I was one of the first guys to say, 'C'mon, guys, let's get our asses back in gear.' You know, business, business, business. Now, looking back, I think that was just my way of dealing with it. Not pretending that it didn't happen, but just trying to put it on the back burner.

"It was overwhelming. I was either at the pile or attending memorials. If I was really lucky, it might be a funeral instead of a memorial.

"The days and weeks after 11 September were a blur. It was funerals, wakes, memorials, going to the firehouse, and then I saw so little of my family. Obviously we were short guys at the firehouse, and by the time you'd get home it would be 2 a.m. You'd have a funeral all next day and then go back to the pile.

"We've all lost friends. I stopped counting at 80-something."

One of Sean's closest friends from Squad 1 was Dave Fontana. Dave's wife, Marian, decided to give Dave a faux funeral with a borrowed empty casket so that their son Aidan would understand that Daddy wasn't coming home. Up until the funeral Aidan had been planning a welcome home party for his dad.

Sean had been scheduled to speak at the funeral, but he was unable to. "I wish we had had more time to find him," he said at the time.

The same weekend, Sean and Maureen headed up to Boston for a memorial for Gerry Dewan. But in a strange twist of fate, the bodies of the two firefighters, linked by their friendship to Sean Cummins, were both found on 6 December.

Sean looks back to the days before 11 September with sorrow. "The Sunday night before it happened, Maureen and the kids were at the beach and Gerry had come upstairs to see me. He wanted to practice some stuff, so we were going over some drills. You know, webbing and strapping and stuff. I was telling him I was going to miss Brooklyn, and you know what he said to me on that Sunday evening? 'There's only one thing you need to know about Manhattan. Manhattan is a doozy.' Unbeknownst to us that 36 hours later the world would have changed.

"Somebody really dropped the ball on this one. This wasn't two little planes out of some place like Mercer airport. These were commercial airliners they hijacked. And what I still can't figure out is why they took so long to figure it was an attack. It's not as if someone could have accidentally hit

the twin towers on 11 September. It was a beautiful day. It's
not as if all of a sudden you come across them. You could see
them for miles, especially on that Tuesday.

"I was driving back across the bridge at about midnight
that Monday night, coming home from the scuba class, and
I had a fantastic view of Manhattan, from the towers right
up to the 90s. It was a beautiful midnight, crystal clear. I
didn't think it would be the last time I saw them."

CHAPTER THIRTEEN

BREEZY POINT

I T IS A bitterly cold and wet Saturday afternoon in Breezy Point, which juts out to sea at the furthest point of the Rockaway peninsula. Breezy, as it is known, is a gated community, with access only through a special security area. It has some of the richest housing in New York, but there are also many working-class families. It is probably one of the most Irish enclaves in the United States, and as firemen and policemen have long resided there, the community was hit very hard on 11 September.

Seated in the rectory of St Vincent's, Father Vincent O'Connell, from Duagh, County Kerry, talks about the toughest period of his life as a priest – counselling those who lost loved ones on 11 September.

"It's very difficult, yet I found there was quite a difference between a memorial where a family did not have a body and a funeral service where they had. Those who found a body felt a sense of tremendous comfort; those who did not found they were having great difficulty obtaining any closure. There is something about being able to put your hand on the coffin of a loved one that makes it easier to accept.

"What do you say to people? I am sorry for your loss? Your son is with God? – to which many have replied to me, 'I want my son with me, not with God.' Obviously there is a lot of anger, very understandably so. The diocese has been sending out grief counsellors and holding team counselling efforts. They have been successful for some, fortunately."

It is clear that discussing the aftermath of 11 September remains painful for him. But he draws some consolation from the fact that he and his fellow priests have made an extraordinary effort to help their traumatised parishioners.

"It helped me enormously to spend a day at Ground Zero, working there. We went to the hotel and were briefed before we went down. We were warned that if it was too difficult that they would come and take any of us away.

"When I was down there we saw parts of bodies, and we realised what they were warning us about. We blessed the firemen and the rescue workers. It was actually a great experience to be there. There was a tremendous unity among those who spent their days there. It was a humbling experience for all of us.

"People are obviously leaning on the church enormously. It is very understandable. They have experienced true evil. They come home to the evil and the suffering every day."

He points out that many on the day could see the twin towers ablaze in the distance from several points around Rockaway. "Now they look and are reminded every time that the towers and their loved ones are no more."

Sister Mary Beata Geraghty, who also ministers in Breezy Point, says that the experience, though horrific, has also had its beneficial side effects. "The community rallying-around has been tremendous. People who lost loves ones were constantly on this community's mind. Everyone is helping: if they need to get dropped somewhere, if they haven't had time to prepare food. I have never seen such closeness."

It is a wet and cold afternoon, with a typical Rockaway gale blowing up outside. The priest and nun were joined by Rose Ellen Dowdell, a striking Italian American woman whose husband of 20 years, Kevin, perished on 11 September. She has come to talk about her husband to a stranger, not because she is seeking consolation, she says, but because it helps her to gather her thoughts about him.

Sleep has been difficult; sometimes the nightmares about what happened to her Kevin in his final moments wake her up in a cold sweat. His body had not been found, but she was reluctant to hold a service for him, saying that it would bring no closure to her.

Captain Kevin Dowdell was a firefighter for 20 years and was one of the most experienced men on the force. "He was very well trained, he's been through a lot of dangerous situations, and I was sure nothing would ever happen to him. He'd always call and say to me after a big fire, 'Before you see it on the news, I'm okay.'

"That day I was in school, I'm a teacher, when the news hit. It is funny, when you are taking a class you are in a cocoon, nothing else seems to matter, then suddenly everything fell apart.

"I had my phone out all morning waiting for him to call me. By 6 o'clock that night I knew it wasn't good. I hadn't heard from him yet, but I did not actually believe it until the fire department called the next day to say he was missing. I thought they must be talking about someone else – he's going to come home, I know it.

"My two sons, Patrick and James, have been my tower of strength. One is in college, the other finishing high school. I'm just glad they spent so many years with Kevin; many of the firemen killed had very young children who will never know their fathers. We have a support group for the wives from the company who lost their husbands. It is tougher if the children are younger, I think.

"Kevin loved the Tyrone Pipe Band. If a new recruit arrived and could play the pipes, Kevin would always try to find a place for him. He was the bass drummer. The two kids also play; James switched from pipes to snare drum, but Patrick stayed with the pipes. It all began when the two boys were taking pipe lessons and Kevin used to drive them there, and he said, 'Why not join them rather than sit out in the car waiting for them?'

"On the Saturday before he died, he took part in the Labor Day parade with the Tyrone pipers. I wanted to see Patrick come up the avenue with the Iona College pipers, so we stayed on until he came past.

"The next day, Sunday, Pat was applying to West Point, and Kevin helped him all that day to prepare his application.

On Sunday night Kevin brought Pat back to school and then he came home. The next day, the tenth, he was going on a 24 hour shift as usual. I remember it so clearly. We talked and he said, 'I'll see you tomorrow.' That was my last conversation with him.

"We met when I was just 18 and he was 20. He was working in the Sandhog union, tunnelling. It was at the Nevins Street subway station. We had a mutual friend and he eventually got my phone number. We started dating in 1980, 21 years ago.

"Now everything has changed; my world has stopped. It is as if I haven't gone forward from that day. Kevin loved Irish music and my sons had put 'Four Green Fields' on his computer, and sometimes it will still play throughout the house, either that or bagpipe stuff that he loved.

"It is a consolation to me that he died a hero, but my greatest consolation is that my children spent enough time with him and that he taught them how to be good men. That is the most positive thing I can take away with me.

"They had a wonderful relationship. During hurricane season the three of them would walk along the beach at Rockaway and find everything that the storm had turned up. The house was full of old bottles and sea glasses.

"Religion has been a great consolation, also the companionship of the other widows. Nine of us in Rescue 4 have lost our husbands, but we genuinely get along well and try to help each other.

"I look back on that fire in Queens on Father's Day, 2001, when the three firemen were killed. I see those wives all the time. We looked at them after it happened to us, as if they had been without their husbands for so long. Then we realised that it was only two months previous. Those girls were still so new to this. This is their first Christmas, birthdays, all that, without their husbands. They have younger children. It is so new for all of us.

"I can't imagine it getting better right now. My two boys are wonderful. They call me every day and tell me about the body counts and they keep me updated. The men from Rescue 4 have been down there every single day. They have found everyone except for Kevin and Peter Brennan, who was with Kevin because he was the newest guy in the company.

"We know what happened to him, I think. When they went to the fire, they parked by City Hall and walked down Broadway, and they stopped at a command post. After that they went over to Liberty Street and stopped at the firehouse because Kevin wanted the layout of the building; then they had to walk along Liberty on the far side of the street because people were jumping.

"When that subsided, they went right into the Trade Center up to the lobby area where the line for the observation decks was. The local elevators only went up to the 40th floor, so we think they decided to take the elevator to the 40th floor and were going to walk up the rest of the way. They found three of the guys right there in the lobby then, and another one of them was found a little bit over, and then one other guy who was a flight up. They think if they don't find Kevin and Pat Brennan, they may have gone outside to a command post.

"How much would it mean if they found him? At first I didn't think it would matter, but it does. I know I'm waiting for it. I need a proper funeral. I don't think it will make me feel better. I won't have a memorial without his body, so I'm still waiting. My sons also want to wait. I live in limbo right now: no way I can go forward and I can't go back. I'm stuck. You get pictures in your head and you can't live with that.

"They really feel they are going to find him. I was down there – it was very comforting to be there. It felt like that was where he was, and I just wanted to be there with him.

"No I'm not angry, it is not in my nature. There is a grieving process I go through. At Christmas we did a Christmas tree, even though we didn't feel like it, because we knew that is what he would want. He never did it anyway. He'd just sit and watch us or play his Irish music. That's what I miss, just the little things. He used to call me all the time, making sure I was okay and the kids were okay."

In mid-April 2002 the family of Kevin Dowdall finally held a memorial service for him, the first chance for the family to achieve some closure.

CHAPTER FOURTEEN

POLICE

LIKE THE FIREMEN, the New York Police Department has its roots in the city's Dutch colonial past. In 1658 the Burgher Guard, a volunteer group of eight night patrolmen to watch for crimes being committed, was established. By 1734, when the city had a population of 10,000, a paid force of 12 men was established.

After the American revolution, a constabulary system and night watch were introduced; and by 1800 a high constable was appointed to govern the police force. John Hayes, the father of the NYPD, held the position for the next 50 years.

By 1845, following the London example, the Municipal Police Act made New York the first city in the United States to adopt a full-time police force as crime began to mount, spawned by a huge influx of immigrants, many of whom in modern times would be called refugees. The Irish soon put their stamp on the police department, as, like the fire service, it represented a way out of the ghetto and a steady and sure income.

By 1850, however, lawlessness was widespread, and New York had more arrests for murder than London. In 1863 the Draft Riots, sparked by angry Irish mobs protesting Civil War conscription, saw two police precincts burned down and 80 officers wounded.

In 1895, the police force came under the iron rule of future president Theodore Roosevelt, who waged war on corruption and ensured that ethnic minorities and women were admitted to the force for the first time. In 1898 the New York Charter consolidated all local forces in the city boroughs into the official NYPD.

In 1918 and 1920, two major landmarks were reached when Ellen O'Grady was appointed the first female deputy commissioner and, two years later, a black policewoman, Lawon R. Bruce, was appointed to the NYPD.

During prohibition, in the 1920s, 57 officers were killed in the line of duty, still the largest number of casualties in any decade. In the 1930s the Seabury Commission found widespread bribery of police and prosecutors. Mayor Jimmy Walker was implicated in the scandal and fled the country.

By the end of the Second World War, when demobilisation occurred, over 23,000 men applied for police positions. The job had become one of the most secure in the country and one that was very highly sought after.

By the 1960s the NYPD, like the rest of America, was changed by the civil rights movement, the race issue and the Vietnam War. In 1968 the American Civil Liberties Union (ACLU) praised the police for how they handled riots following the death of Martin Luther King. In efforts to have the police force be more representative, it was mandated that nearly 25 per cent of the police recruits be drawn from minority groups. The modern day evolution of the NYPD into a force of 38,000 police officers, drawn from every racial group and representing the largest city force in the country, had begun.

The crack epidemic in the 1980s pushed the murder rate to the highest point in history. Soon after, new policing techniques, relying heavily on computer pinpointing of serious crime areas, began to drive the statistics down. Under Mayor Rudy Giuliani, they fell to 1960s levels.

Thus, as the new millennium dawned, both the fire and police services of New York had largely met the extraordinary challenges of keeping one of the largest and most diverse cities in the world as safe as possible. Through two centuries the men and women of the FDNY and the NYPD had faced many trials and overcome even the most difficult of them. Countless thousands of lives had been saved by their brave actions, and they had developed a worldwide reputation for being the best at what they did.

Yet their greatest challenge was still to confront them.

CHAPTER FIFTEEN

IN THE LINE OF FIRE

SERGEANT NOEL FIRTH well remembers his first day in the Police Academy in New York in July of 1988. The attractive fellow rookie he met on that day, Moira Reddy, was like him the child of Irish immigrants and determined to be a top cop. "She was always smiling, laughing, easygoing, but you knew she was serious behind it all. She wanted to get ahead in the job."

It wasn't easy being a female in a still overwhelmingly male profession, but Moira had learned from her parents and her Brooklyn upbringing just how to take care of herself.

Moira and Noel both graduated in December of 1988, and they ended up as transit cops, policing the subways which back then had very high crime rates. "She was active," is what Firth remembers, the ultimate compliment. "She was a good cop who was always on top of things."

Then, on 28 August 1991, the worst subway accident in 63 years occurred on their beat. Five people were killed and more than 200 injured when a southbound No. 4 train ran a red light and derailed just north of Union Square. The motorman, Robert Ray, who was subsequently proven to have been drunk at the time of the accident, was speeding at 40 miles per hour on a slow stretch of track where the speed limit was only 10 mph. He was later convicted of manslaughter and sentenced to 15 years in prison.

For Noel Firth and Moira Reddy, who were among the first to the site of the wreck, the damage done looked catastrophic. Through an extraordinary foul-up, the electricity was not turned off, which meant that the third rail was live. As they were splashing around in water, it was very hazardous, but Firth and Reddy did not hesitate to throw themselves into the rescue effort.

"There were an awful lot of people dazed, several seriously hurt and many we knew we could do nothing for," Firth recalls. He remembers one man in particular, who was pinned between the roof of the tunnel and the top of the subway car. Despite their best efforts they could not reach him.

But they saved many other lives. They spent much of the night ferrying people out from under the subway wreckage to safety. He remembers Reddy's "extraordinary courage" and her willingness to go back again and again to save people. "She was one brave cop," he says now. For her efforts she was awarded the Distinguished Duty Medal. Three years later she was in the news again when she helped rescue several people when a bomb exploded in a subway car on Fulton Street.

Moira Ann Reddy had always shown a special kind of dedication to getting the job done and helping others. She was born in Brooklyn on Valentine's Day, 14 February 1963, to John Reddy from Dublin and Mary Finn. She had one sister, Mary Elizabeth.

From age five when she went to kindergarten in PS 170 with her best friend Kathleen Conaghan, Moira was the centre of attention, and already an activist. In fifth grade at Our Lady of Perpetual Help in Sunset Park, she petitioned the parish priest to allow women to be altar servers, says her friend Cathy Gallogoly.

While other kids played with dolls and Barbie toys, Moira loved spy games and pretending she was a cop pursuing criminals. She particularly enjoyed stakeouts, her friends remember. "As teenagers we were Charlie's Angels, me, Moira and Cathy," says her childhood friend Kathleen. "'Oh, come on, you guys, you want to be cops when you grow up, don't you?' she would say." They didn't, but she did.

Perhaps it was because her neighbourhood was full of

serving and retired cops, but early on in her life she informed everyone that she was going to join the NYPD. At the time it was an unusual ambition for a woman.

On St Patrick's Day, Moira was the most enthusiastic Irish person in the neighbourhood. Once while the young friends were making their way to the parade, she bought a button saying "Honorary Irishman". When she found out what "Honorary" meant, she was disgusted and ripped it off.

"When you looked at Moira you knew right off that she was Irish," Officer Paul Adams told the *Daily News*: "strawberry blonde, blue eyes, fair skin and the gift of the gab."

In September of 1981, Moira set out for Niagara University along with her friend Kathleen. The college, on the edge of the US/Canadian border in the frozen north of the state, was a major change from Brooklyn and New York City, but her friends say Moira soon warmed the place up. But even after graduation and work in the travel business, she was still determined to become a cop.

She fulfilled her dream in 1988. "She loved being a police officer and thrived in that position," says her niece and goddaughter Allison Reddy. "She always ended her conversations by saying 'I love you,' so we were never left in doubt, because she put her life on the line just by being in that uniform."

Moira was working at Transit Police District 4 when she met a cop called Jim Smith. She introduced herself by taking off his Yankee hat and throwing it across the room.

Their first date was Valentine's Day 1992. They went to a New York Rangers' game. As Jim recalls, they both fell in love, he with her and she with one of the Rangers' players. Thus began their love affair, which culminated in marriage in May of 1998.

They honeymooned in Maui, Hawaii, and Jim remembers a woman who above all loved to travel and experience the world to the full. She ran with the bulls in Spain, played roulette in Monte Carlo and rode a camel in North Africa. But she loved nothing better than to drag friends and family off on trips around the US in her Winnebago van. "Her idea of a romantic holiday was to bring six or seven people instead of the usual 15," says Jim.

On 20 July 1999, Moira gave birth to Patricia Mary. It was the happiest day of her life. Right from the beginning, her friends say, she was besotted with her baby. Her life, with a career she loved and a happy marriage and beautiful child, seemed complete.

Then came 11 September.

Smith was among the first cops to report that a plane had flown into the World Trade Center and that she was on her way there with her partner. Once there she immediately began helping people to safety in the most dangerous of circumstances. She never backed off, even for a moment. "Honour and duty required it; Moira's personal faith demanded it," says her husband.

James Smith has learned that his wife led countless people out of the wreckage on the day. There is now a famous photograph of Moira leading a bleeding man to safety before heading back into the inferno.

She was in tower two, and despite the enormous danger, she kept at her job. A trader with the firm Eurobrokers later recalled her as "intense but calm", her blue eyes steady, her voice very even. "Don't look, keep moving," she kept telling people as bodies crashed all around them and the building began to fall apart. Because of her commands, people kept moving where otherwise they would have been frozen in terror. She is credited with saving scores of lives.

When the towers collapsed, Moira Smith was still in radio contact, but soon all contact ceased. Despite a massive search, her body was not recovered. As her colleague Lisa Novarro says, "Fearless might not be the right word, but it is the first to come to mind. It is little wonder how she spent her last moments. The picture in the paper showed her to be alive. She could have saved herself, but nothing would have stopped her saving one more person. I'm not sure hero is the perfect word, but it is the first one that comes to mind."

She was 38 years old.

On a frigid, windy but sun-filled February day, over five months after 11 September, the memorial service for Police

Officer Moira Smith was finally held. Over 10,000 police
officers of every rank and station filled St Patrick's Cathedral
to overflowing and spilled over outside.

Before entering the church they had lined up in serried
file for blocks along Fifth Avenue, forcing the busy Valentine's Day traffic to a grinding halt. Everywhere you looked,
there was a sea of blue uniforms and white gloves, broken
only by an incongruous splash of red, worn by a delegation
from the Royal Canadian Mounted Police.

In front of the church the bagpipe band of the Emerald
Society took their places. At the head of the band, the flags
of the United States, Ireland and of the state of New York
were borne by the standard bearers. Each member of the
band wore a sprig of green in his beret. The cadence of a single muffled drum beat out across the avenue, marking time
until the service began.

As the officers filed past on their way into the church, it
seemed every second officer had an Irish surname. Fahey,
Murphy, Hynes, O'Brien, Clarke, Maguire, FitzPatrick,
Curtin: the list went on and on. They were the sons and
daughters and descendants of thousands of Irish immigrants
who had risked the Atlantic passage to find a new life in
America. Like many of their forefathers, the policemen were
drawn into the force by the ethnic ties and family bonding
which is an unbreakable part of the New York Police Department tradition.

The brotherhood and sisterhood of police officers was
also on display. They came from London, Toronto, California and Massachusetts, from Florida, Alabama and Col-
orado. When an officer goes down, the nationwide
community of police treats it like the death of one of their
own.

Few can memorialise their own like the NYPD. They
have had far more practice at it than any other police service
in America, perhaps the world, and they carry it out to per-
fection. The honour guard, the bagpipers, the VIPs and family members of the deceased all play their part in a
well-choreographed script. But even they, on this occasion,
found it hard to stick to the spit and polish.

For all of them there was the heartbreaking sight of Patricia Smith, all of two years old, carried into the church by her father, Officer James Smith, Moira's husband. She was wearing a green velvet dress and had a giddy smile on her face from all the attention. There was an impish air about her, as there is with all two-year-olds. Relatives, friends and policemen formed a protective cocoon around Moira's husband and daughter as they made their way up the aisle.

Every time the closed-circuit cameras caught the little girl during the services, there was a collective intake of breath, and many of the most hardened members of the NYPD wiped away tears. At one point she wandered up and down the aisles, smiling at faces she knew, and the camera caught her laughing face as she shook her brown curly hair.

Edward Cardinal Egan, who had been criticised by many for departing for Rome and staying there for almost a month right after 11 September, was taking no chances on missing this service, the most high profile in months.

Bidding everyone welcome he went over the details of Moira Smith's life, her dedication and her courage and her selfless nature which cost her her life. He talked about her love for her daughter and the fact that she was being memorialised on Valentine's Day, her 39th birthday. An impressive speaker, Egan easily held the congregation's attention as did her niece and two lifelong friends and a policewoman colleague who spoke after him.

However, it was Police Commissioner Ray Kelly who caught the bravery of the missing woman best. Kelly pointed out that Moira Smith had been miles away from Ground Zero when the planes hit, but she had rushed to the scene and helped victims before returning to her precinct and organising another group of rescuers. That group included herself and her partner Robert Fazio, who would both lose their lives.

Kelly said it was not a surprise that Smith went back in again and again. She had already proven her bravery several times during her career. "No words can comfort her family now, but we pledge to honour her memory by never forgetting her," he said.

Jim Smith remembered his wife's love for their daughter and how they had all watched the *Wizard of Oz* together hundreds of times. It was only after Moira's death that he had come to appreciate one of the morals of that much-beloved tale.

"The Wizard told the Tin Man that a heart is not judged by how much you love, but by how much you were loved by others," he said, adding that judging by the massive attendance Moira must have been loved indeed.

Referring to the fact that a commuter boat that plies the New York waterways had just been named for Moira, Smith stated: "On the side of the *Moira Smith* is a Claddagh, an Irish symbol meaning friendship, loyalty, and love. This design embodies what Moira means to us: a good friend, a loyal police officer and American, and the love of our lives. There is a traditional saying that goes with the giving of a Claddagh: 'With these hands I give you my heart, and I crown it with my love.' God bless Moira, and God bless all those who gave their lives in this fight for freedom. Thank you."

Afterwards, Governor George Pataki and Mayor Michael Bloomberg finished their eulogies, and the strains of "God Bless America" carried out on to the streets outside. The dignitaries and the 10,000 cops streamed out of the service and lined up opposite the church. Then, as a hush fell, the family came outside and faced the honour guard.

The trumpet players, perched on a stand across the street in the shadow of the Rockefeller Center, played the "Last Post", and a perfect silence followed on Fifth Avenue for a few fleeting moments.

Then with loving care and no little ceremony, the American flag was carried to the family and presented to the little girl and her father. She looked up at her daddy as he held the flag for her, her little hand grasping one corner of it, a quizzical look on her face.

After the flag bearer saluted and resumed his position, the family was brought to the waiting limousine, and the top brass of the department, the dignitaries and the politicians all followed in line. Then with a single drum beating, the

NYPD Emerald Society pipes and drums led the procession down Fifth Avenue, past the six blocks of mourners and police.

Through the limousine window, Patricia Mary, sitting on her father's lap, waved to all the police as her father kissed her curls. Finally the cortège moved slowly out of sight.

As the mourners dispersed, the late afternoon temperature dropped to near freezing and a chill wind blew from the east. Over five months after the 11 September attacks, yet another father finally faced life without his beloved wife, and a little girl with sparkling eyes and brown curls was left without her mother.

Moira Smith's body was finally found in mid-March 2002, not far from where she had last been seen saving lives. Thousands attended her funeral.

CHAPTER SIXTEEN

BRUCE REYNOLDS

POLICE OFFICER BRUCE Reynolds, one of the 37 members of the Port Authority Police Department who perished on 11 September, had recently returned from his annual summer sojourn in Ireland – County Donegal, to be specific.

While there Bruce enjoyed long walks by the sea with his wife Marian and two young children, Brianna and Michael. His serious love of the great outdoors meant that he spent most of his time in Ireland outside, rain or shine. Cutting turf in a peat bog, trimming hedges that needed tending to on the family farm or just relishing quiet time breathing in the pure Donegal air – Bruce just couldn't get enough.

At night, with a satisfying day's work behind him and the kids tucked into bed, Bruce would visit the local pub for a few pints and maybe a sing-song – old Irish ballads were a particular Reynolds specialty.

Bruce Reynolds, though, wasn't the typical Irish immigrant returning home from the hustle and bustle of America to catch up with family and friends on a summer vacation. Far from it.

Bruce Reynolds, only 41 when he died, was black. He was born in Pittsburgh and raised in Manhattan in a proud black household. But Bruce's heart unquestionably belonged to Ireland.

"Bruce," says his father, J.A. Reynolds, "was more Irish than the Irish themselves."

His 31 July 1993 marriage to Donegal native Marian
McBride ensured that a virtually lifelong affinity for the Irish
would continue for the rest of his life. But no one could have
envisaged just how short his life would be or the emotional
devastation his senseless death would leave behind.

J.A. Reynolds, 78, and his wife Geri, 76, are alone again,
just as they were when they married over 50 years ago. Their
beloved Bruce was an only child, and the Reynolds doted on
him like he was the only person in the world. Yet the couple
readily admit that there were things they didn't really know
about their son. Not bad things: Bruce had wanted to be a
police officer since he was a little boy and always had a great
respect for the law. And don't all kids hide something or
other about themselves from their parents?

In a way, the pleasant discoveries J.A. and Geri are
making about their son almost amount to a rebirth of a new
Bruce, a Bruce his parents are anxious to get to know. The
facets of Bruce's life that he kept to himself have proven to
be a source of endless wonder and curiosity for the couple,
who are on a mission to find out as much as they can about
the child who was the light of their lives.

For J.A. and Geri, Bruce has become almost more of an
obsession in death than he was in life. Their cosy one-
bedroom apartment in the Inwood section of Manhattan is
dominated with Bruce memorabilia and a multitude of letters
and cards from both friends and strangers mourning his loss.
The meticulous J.A. will shortly organise it all into a huge
binder and a huge photo mural, about five feet long, of pictures of Bruce, dominated by ones taken the weekend before
his death on a family outing to the Bronx Zoo to celebrate
little Brianna's fourth birthday.

Like so many families who lost a loved one on 11 September, J.A. Reynolds, months later, has found it enormously difficult to let go, especially since Bruce's body has
yet to be found. "At this point in my life I'm trying to find
closure," he says. "The thing is, I know where Bruce was,
but I don't know where he is now. It's taken me a long time
to accept that Bruce isn't coming back . . . but I'm still not
sure about that.

"The reason is is that his presence is so strong. His presence in this room, it's still here. You know, Bruce was always here – he didn't leave until he got married at 33 years of age. And he was always here after that. I've needed time to just reflect on Bruce, and I need to be uncluttered mentally and emotionally to deal with what's happened. I feel very strongly about the mural I'm doing, just putting the pictures together, and I'm working on a lot of other things, too.

"I've been doing a lot of reflecting on the memorial mass that was held for Bruce in New Jersey. It was one of the most beautiful masses that I ever attended. In my mind I'm working on capturing the feeling of the mass. It was so totally Irish. The feeling and the mood, and the voices and the sounds of Irish lilts, it was amazing to me. Here they had this picture of a black man enlarged on the altar, and everything around it was so Irish. Yet it made so much sense. It wasn't some strange novelty that a black man rather than an Irishman was being celebrated."

When looking back at the life and times of J.A., Geri and Bruce Reynolds, it's not at all surprising that the Irish embraced Bruce as one of their own. Diversity was something that J.A. and Geri cherished, often against the odds. America is rightfully spoken of as the greatest nation in the world, but its history is littered with discrimination and racism against blacks that in some quarters continues unabated to this day.

That didn't stop the Reynolds family from trying to realise their own American dream. Originally from Pittsburgh, J.A., Geri and five-year-old Bruce moved to New York in 1965, prompted by the passage of civil rights laws a year earlier that nudged open the doors of opportunity for blacks. J.A. was doing fine working in the personnel department of a major gas company, and Geri was employed as a social worker. Still, the money wasn't great and the prospects for advancement practically nil.

"When the civil rights laws passed, I thought New York City would give me better advantages," J.A. recalls. "I had visited the city several times before for interviews before I left my company in Pittsburgh.

"I was also very interested in the theatre and interested in performing. I had actually hoped to make that my major source of income, so that had a lot to do with our decision to move as well."

The young family made what could be considered an odd choice at the time – they relocated to a section of Manhattan known as Inwood, a small, quiet enclave located at the northern tip of the city filled with Irish, Italians, Jews and other non-black ethnic groups. A couple of J.A.'s friends drove him around the city to find a new home, but instead of settling in Harlem, the traditional black hub, he took an instant liking to Inwood. The one-bedroom apartment located on the sixth floor of the complex they settled in, with a view of the Harlem River to the east, is the same one J.A. and Geri still reside in today.

"There was some apprehension because we were the first black family in Inwood, so there was some hesitancy," J.A. says. "I didn't take it seriously, and I wasn't afraid. We had lived in a mixed neighbourhood in Pittsburgh. I would have been more apprehensive moving into a totally ethnic community like Harlem."

"It didn't really dawn on us that there would be a problem. We had always thought of New York as a big melting pot," Geri adds. Still, there were teething problems. New York City may be a sophisticated metropolis, but diversity isn't always accepted.

Geri decided to test the level of tolerance of her new neighbours the first week she and J.A. and Bruce moved in. A playground in Isham Park, just down the street from the apartment on Park Terrace West, was the first port of call she made with her young son. Some of the locals weren't overjoyed when they caught sight of the new kid on the block.

"Hardly anyone played with him," Geri says. "And the people were so aloof. I couldn't allow this to happen to my child, so I said to myself that I had to do something about it. We were married several years before we had Bruce, so everyone just showered him with everything back in Pittsburgh. He had the most wonderful toys you could ever want, and he had a little red wagon. So the next day I took some of his toys, put them in the wagon and walked down to the playground.

"Well, the kids just flocked to him," Geri laughs. "They made friends with Bruce, and I made friends, too. Even the kids who played at the park were in some ways separated from each other. So I'd have Rebecca on one side of me and Mary on the other, and I'd say, 'Rebecca, do you know Mary?' So they became friends, too. After six months we had so many friends between us that we couldn't count them. Bruce got invited to all the birthday parties, bar mitzvahs, you name it."

"It was probably hard for the neighbours," J.A. adds. "Some thought, when they saw one black family coming in, they thought, well, there goes the neighbourhood. But we were not connected in that way. We were individuals."

The Reynolds completely immersed themselves in their new surroundings, even opening their home on Christmas Day for a big open house party for their new friends. J.A. was employed by the city, and Geri was a happy mom who made sure her Bruce was well looked after.

Bruce and Geri went to great lengths to ensure that the harsh consequences of racism never set foot at their door.

"In the time I grew up in, the 1920s and thirties, Bruce would have been beaten up and really badly mistreated," says J.A. "But the important thing is to allow things to change, instead of hanging back in the past. So we did things to prevent Bruce from being mistreated by his peers.

"I soon realised that Inwood was very turf-oriented. There were gangs that dominated Isham Park, white gangs, predominantly Irish, some Italians, so this worried us. And if another group of kids went into their territory, they would get beat up. My greatest fear before moving to New York was that Bruce would get wrongly involved with a gang."

J.A. and Geri joined the Inwood Civic Council, which was made up of mostly older white folks. Geri became involved with the parent-teacher group at Bruce's public school, but most important, the Reynolds decided to form a "gang" of their own, figuring if you can't beat 'em, you might as well join 'em.

The new Park Terrace West gang wasn't interested in fighting or protecting their turf, though. The adults, led by J.A. and Geri, formulated a programme of activities for the kids to keep them happily occupied and out of the sinister clutches of the more threatening elements of the community. The government of New York City chipped in some funds which allowed the Park Terrace West gang to take over a run-down corner of Isham Park and transform it into a sparkling little oasis of tranquillity. The bit of land they took over came to be known as "Bruce's garden".

"That's really what Bruce was involved in – cleaning up the park," says Geri. "That's what he really loved. Soon everybody started to get involved in the park and preserving it – young people and senior citizens. The young people helped the older ones develop gardens within the gardens. It became quite a neighbourhood thing. The kids would go there after school and feel safe."

The Park Terrace West gang took on a vibrant life of its own, and eventually its members, Bruce among them, peacefully confronted those in the "evil" gangs in an effort to make them realise that violence didn't pay. "Bruce really went in among them," remembers Geri. "He tried to teach them that the gardens and the park belonged to them, too, and how important it was to preserve and share them."

Instead of hanging out on street corners looking for trouble, the Park Terrace West members spent their free time going to Broadway shows, listening to lectures from police officers and, of course, tending to the park. Bruce was always in the middle of it all, the popular one. No one dared say anything even remotely hostile to Bruce Reynolds, for he had a posse of friends who were always ready to stick up for him.

"Bruce just loved growing up here," Geri says. "He had lots and lots of good friends."

The Reynolds were typical parents in every way. They enrolled their son in a series of private schools, obtaining for him the best education that money could buy, and they stayed awake at night when their son was out, until they heard his key turn in the door. The single bedroom in the apartment was given to their adored only child; J.A. and Geri slept on a pull-out sofa in the living room. There were no sacrifices that Mr and Mrs Reynolds wouldn't make for Bruce.

The allure of the plants and trees just outside their doorstep was irresistible to the Reynolds family. "When Bruce was young, I took him to the woods in autumn to collect leaves," recalls J.A. "We would bring them home in bouquets and compare their colour to our skin tones. We would compare the oak leaves to Bruce, and we'd compare them to his mother's colouring and to mine."

Bruce was a good student, which wasn't at all surprising given the importance his parents placed on education. Both the Reynolds were accomplished professionals in their own right: after working for the city, J.A. took a job at the Fashion Institute of Technology, and Geri wrote a column on family matters for a local publication.

Still, J.A. was shocked when his son revealed his career plans. He wanted to be a police officer. J.A. was perplexed by the choice, given how much money and effort he had invested in his son's education, and he readily admits that he was not pleased.

Geri remembers Bruce talking about his desire to be a cop as early as his eighth birthday, but children so young rarely have a concept as to what they want to do with the rest of their lives, so the Reynolds shrugged it off. Bruce graduated from the Fashion Institute of Technology with a degree in advertising communications, but he had no intention of entering the corporate world.

"We were disappointed. I did everything I did with his education to get him to pursue other things," says J.A. "I felt being a cop was a very dangerous job. I couldn't picture Bruce as a police officer; I didn't see him as being that physical. It's a very demanding job, especially when you have to deal with a perpetrator, and I didn't see Bruce as being the tough guy. I didn't see him as a combative person."

"He told me that he wanted to be a police officer since he was eight years old," Geri recalls. "He said, 'Mom, you and Dad can be the students. You and Dad are the social workers. Maybe my kids will be someday, but not me.'"

Bruce Reynolds took the exams for both the New York Police Department and the Port Authority Police Force and scored high marks on both tests. The Port Authority oversees law enforcement for New York and New Jersey's vast infrastructure system, including all the bridges, tunnels and roads. Bruce chose the Port Authority over the city's police department because the pay was better and the job was in many ways less risky.

He officially joined the force in 1986, and he was extremely happy. He was involved in all kinds of different beats. Ironically, he was called to the scene of the 1993 bombing of the World Trade Center, as the Trade Center was a Port Authority-owned property. Before 11 September Bruce's beat was the George Washington Bridge, the double-deckered span called the "GW" by locals which links upper Manhattan to New Jersey.

"It was a job that he really loved," says Geri. "He was very popular with his peers, and it was an incredible experience for him."

As J.A. and Geri Reynolds always knew, Bruce's connections to Ireland were a dominating facet of his life. In the emotionally agonising weeks and months after 11 September, the elderly black couple took plenty of solace from many surprising discoveries as to how Irish their son really was. As they say, the only way he could have been "more" Irish is if he had actually been born there.

His wife Marian McBride, of course, nurtured Bruce's Irish side in so many ways. The Reynolds are clearly devoted to their Irish daughter-in-law, and they're completely crazy about their two grandchildren in the special way that's unique to grandparents. Yet there were many blanks in Bruce's Irish life – several of them simple ones – that his parents haven't been able to fill in throughout the years, for no reason in particular. It's just the way that Bruce was.

"Much of what I'm discovering about Bruce these days are things he never discussed with us," says J.A. "I don't really know why. Some of the things I'd always meant to ask him about, but just never did."

J.A. and Geri aren't really sure when Bruce and Marian

first met or how they became a couple. Their first encounter
with Marian came on Thanksgiving in the early 1990s. Bruce
invited his parents to dinner with his girlfriend at the Green-
tree restaurant in the heavily Irish Riverdale section of the
Bronx.

"Bruce said to me, 'Mom, you're really going to like her.
She's a lady, just like you,' recalls Geri. "And he was right.
We did like her. We liked her very much right from the start."

Marian's mother and twin sister eventually travelled to
New York to meet the Reynolds. Though the two families
were raised an ocean apart and were steeped in completely
different cultures, they couldn't have gotten along better. "It
was like we had known each other our whole lives," says
Geri.

The families exchanged gifts and stories. The visit coin-
cided with Mrs McBride's birthday, so Geri specially ordered
a cake from a Dominican bakery noted for its confectionery.
Mrs McBride, instead of eating the offering, was so chuffed
by the gesture that she chose to bring the cake back to Donegal at the end of her trip for all the family back there to
enjoy.

"We froze it for her, and she carried it on the plane," says
Geri. "When they landed back home it was perfectly thawed.
So there were all these people in Donegal eating a Domini-
can-made cake from New York!"

Marian had also brought Bruce back to meet her family
in Donegal prior to their engagement. J.A. remembers being
quite apprehensive about the visit at the time.

"I was concerned about the colour issue," he says. "But
I didn't say anything to him or Marian. But I had hoped that
Bruce wasn't going into a difficult scene, unaware of what
could happen. With me, coming from the 1920s, I'm always
aware of that thing happening."

J.A. needn't have worried. The McBrides heartily accepted Bruce as one of their own, as did the locals in Donegal.
His father was relieved, to say the least. "Oh yes, I was so
thrilled, so happy to realise that Donegal was the way it is,"
he says.

Given his law enforcement background, Bruce made it a

point to visit Irish police and fire departments. "And they rolled out the red carpet for him," J.A. says.

Marian's father Peter found he had a soulmate in his future son-in-law. The two would spend time in the woodlands and in the peat bogs, working the land and doing whatever needed to be done to keep it in tip-top shape.

Bruce and Marian wed in the summer of 1993 at a Catholic church on Manhattan's West Side, and again a contingent of McBrides from Donegal made the trip for the ceremony and the reception in nearby Hackensack, New Jersey, that followed.

"It was a real Irish wedding, lots of Irish people," says Geri. "Everything was perfect. Marian's brother took part in the ceremony, and so did I and Mrs McBride. Bruce and Marian were so happy."

The couple eventually settled in a big house on lots of land in western New Jersey, down by the Delaware River Gap, almost 100 miles from Bruce's old Inwood stomping grounds where he had lived with his parents until the day he married. Though it was far from home and work, being there allowed Bruce to indulge his love of nature and the outdoors in a way living in the big city never permitted. There's a little pathway off the land where geese and ducks rested, and, of course, Bruce maintained a perfect garden.

Adding to the happiness of Bruce and Marian Reynolds was the addition of their two children. Brianna came on the scene in September 1997; little Michael followed in July 2000.

Being grandparents is one of the great joys in the lives of J.A. and Geri Reynolds, one that has also greatly helped to sustain their spirits since 11 September. They saw their grandchildren fairly regularly, more than would seem possible given the commuting distance. Both Bruce and Marian felt it was important to keep the link.

Bruce would sometimes call his folks at 5 a.m. to ask for babysitting assistance – maybe the babysitter wasn't available or Marian wasn't feeling well, and could he possibly drop the kids off? Those calls always delighted J.A. and Geri, despite the early hour. Brianna and Michael would arrive in

Inwood at 6.30 in their dad's car, and stay for a night or two as well.

The kids love to turn the small living room into a swimming pool, throwing the couch cushions on to the floor and using the frame itself as a diving board. "They have a great time here," laughs J.A. "We basically let them do what they want and don't bother them. And the neighbours come in and play with them, so they're really happy when they're here."

The children, particularly Brianna, being older, were well steeped in Irishness. Michael made his first trip to Ireland in the summer of 2001, but Brianna is a veteran traveller. She even spent nine weeks in Donegal with her mom's family in the summer of 2000 – six were on her own, three with her parents.

"She's been in Ireland every year of her life, so she knows her Irish family quite well," says J.A. "She speaks a little Gaelic, too, and can say prayers in Irish. And she has a ritual with her grandfather. Every morning they would go for a walk by the ocean, and they'd go through the town, and everyone in the town knows Brianna. She's sort of like the boss, you know!"

"Definitely," agrees Geri. "She's known around the town as the princess of Donegal. She just loves it there."

Bruce, Marian and their children had returned from their last vacation to Donegal on 28 August 2001. They had a great time, as they always did, and planned to celebrate Brianna's fourth birthday when they came home. The young family spent the weekend prior to 11 September at the Bronx Zoo for Brianna's big day on 8 September, and had a party to boot. Life couldn't have been better for the young family.

Understandably, the events of 11 September – specifically, what J.A. and Geri experienced – were gut-wrenching for the couple to talk about. It was a gorgeous late summer day in the city, and J.A., being politically and civic minded, was involved in the local elections that had been scheduled. He had given his support to José Torres, a candidate for a city council seat, and he had spent the early morning hours passing out flyers touting Torres' accomplishments to commuters boarding the subway to work.

J.A. remembers someone telling him on his way home that something terrible had happened at the World Trade Center, so when he arrived back he turned on his TV. By that time the second plane had hit, and J.A. instantly thought of his son, but not with any immediate sense of panic, as Bruce would have been working at the GW, far away from the twin towers.

Still, J.A. was aware that his son had been called to the scene of the 1993 bomb attack on the towers, so he called the Port Authority to check on Bruce's whereabouts. Marian, who was working at the time, was doing her own checks as well.

"I called the Port Authority, and whoever answered the phone was very hesitant, and then finally told me Bruce was down there," says J.A. "So I kept calling and calling back to try and find information, and someone told me that Bruce had been injured and taken away on a stretcher to St Vincent's Hospital."

Those words were music to the ears of J.A. and Geri Reynolds. There were reports of thousands of people losing their lives on the dreadful day, and if Bruce was hospitalised it meant that, at least, he was one of the lucky ones who had survived.

Their relief was soon replaced with dread, as there was no record of Bruce being admitted to St Vincent's. J.A. was told that his son might have been taken to another hospital for treatment in New Jersey, but frantic searches turned up no record of a Police Officer Bruce Reynolds.

"I was really hysterical when they couldn't find Bruce," says J.A. "Then I got in touch with Bruce's best friend, who was a police officer, and he told me the same thing about the hospital, and then someone else told me that he had been seen walking up Vesey Street. Then after a couple of days I demanded to go inside the church right by the twin towers. I thought that maybe Bruce had ducked in there for safety. The police told me they had gone through the church, but they'd do it again. Then I thought maybe he was in one of the tunnels that lead into the World Trade Center.

"There was all kinds of hysteria in the days right afterwards. The Port Authority called the next day to apologise for telling me that he was in the hospital. They had told Marian the same thing, too."

The healing process of so suddenly losing a loved one will continue for ever for all the Reynolds. There were several memorials and services in Bruce's memory, and a mass in Paramus, New Jersey, in October. The McBride family travelled from Donegal, and Bruce's friends came from near and far.

J.A. has found comfort in talking to Bruce's friends, which has allowed him to learn more about the son who, in some ways, he didn't really know. "Little things, like he had obtained a financial analyst's licence we didn't know about, and he also tried a catering business up around the Yonkers area. That's not really surprising, because our Bruce loved his food so much – I even wanted to caution him about his poor diet!" says J.A., a slim, fit man who looks younger than his 78 years, no doubt due to the many hours he spends working out at the local gym.

The Reynolds also received a letter from a woman called Joy Mullins, who read about Bruce's death in a story in the *Irish Voice* newspaper at the end of 2001. Ms Mullins used to manage an Irish bar called O'Brien's in upstate Rockland County frequented by Bruce.

"He came in with other young people and was at first very quiet," Ms Mullins wrote. "As he came in more, he became one of my favourite customers. He would sing along with the bands to every Irish song. He was always the most polite young man I had ever met. We became quite friendly, and we would chat about how he loved all Irish things. There were truly times I thought he was more Irish than I – I was born in Ireland and raised there. When I became very busy, Bruce would get me ice and carry up beer cases or whatever else I needed at the time. He was a wonderful young man. I console myself with the fact that all the people I love and respect are together in heaven, hopefully having a pint and singing a good old Irish ditty. I know that if this is true, then your son Bruce is right in the middle, leading everyone on."

Marian, according to Geri, is doing "fair". The holiday season of 2001 was a blur – she dropped her children off with Geri and J.A. for Thanksgiving, unable to cope with the day herself. Christmas was equally painful.

Michael, not even 14 months when his world changed for ever, has little comprehension of what happened. Brianna has shown a maturity far beyond her four years.

"She and her daddy were very close," says Geri. "She expresses her grief very well. She says that a plane flew into a building and that her daddy was hurt, they took him away on a stretcher to hospital and then he went to heaven."

J.A. expresses concern about his grandchildren's future. They live with their Irish mother a good distance from Manhattan, and he frets that the black side of their beings will somehow diminish with time.

"I don't think that Bruce will be forgotten about for a long time, but I do think it will be forgotten that he comes from a black family, and that worries me," says J.A. "Marian was born and raised in Donegal. I feel it's important for us to keep a presence because of the children. Because somewhere down the line they must not forget that they were also black, for their own emotional security.

"I had many friends who were of mixed-parent heritage, and along the way the two-parent connection was broken, and the kids weren't as happy as they could be. One part was missing, and that makes me worry. When death comes as it did to us, sometimes families can become so isolated, so it's my hope to continue a presence in Brianna and Michael's lives. I feel that as the months go by, Marian will become so involved in her Irish culture that the black might get forgotten about.

"I'm hopeful Marian feels the same way. She is just a wonderful, marvellous person. She sometimes would keep the family more together than Bruce would. He'd be too busy with work, or fishing and doing things with his house, but she'd always make sure he'd call home and visit."

Geri Reynolds, a truly lovely woman who remains a rock of strength despite losing her son and suffering from severe arthritis that has twisted her hands and feet for 36 years, is the optimist in the family, the one who maybe, hopefully, sees somewhat brighter days ahead.

"We'll never get over it. With time it might feel a little better, I hope, but there's no getting over it. It's not a solace or anything, but there are so many other 11 September families who are in the same position as we are. We're all suffering together."

CHAPTER SEVENTEEN

DEATH OF A DREAM

ANGELA O'REILLY DANZ, 34, emigrated to the States in her early twenties, and in February of 1987 she met a handsome New York trainee cop at Buckley's Irish pub in East Hampton, the wealthy paradise on Long Island for the rich and famous. Angela was in the Hamptons working as an au pair for a family, and Vincent, an ex-marine who was the youngest of nine children, had just started as a cadet in the Police Academy.

On the night they first laid eyes on each other they instantly clicked, and Angela says that she knew from the get-go that Vincent Danz would one day be her husband. "I told him when I met him I was going to marry him. He just threw his head back and laughed at me," Angela fondly remembers. "I knew the minute I laid eyes on him. He was a funny individual. He was very charismatic."

Vincent introduced Angela to all the finer points of life as a New Yorker. The two toured New York City from top to bottom, and the young officer loved sharing his knowledge of all of Manhattan's riches with his immigrant girlfriend. Vincent taught Angela how to navigate the city's complex subway system and even helped her understand the value of American dollars, vis-à-vis Irish punts.

Angela may have been sure she'd met her match, but the couple dated for two years before tying the knot in a small summer ceremony in 1989 for family and friends in Southampton, another Long Island enclave on the Atlantic favoured by summer revellers. She remembers the ceremony as being full of fun and love, the perfect way to start what was supposed to have been a perfect life together.

Angela and Vincent Danz couldn't have been happier, and their joy was sealed with the birth of their first daughter, Winifred, now aged nine. When Emily came along three years later, Angela left her job at Salomon, Smith and Barney, a Manhattan-based investment house. Their youngest, Abigail, was born at the start of 2001. Ireland was very close to Angela's heart.

Raising her children in her native Dublin alongside her family was always Angela's dream, but Vincent Danz, 38, had a thriving career in the department and no desire to make the trans-Atlantic trek. It was the one small bone of contention between the couple, but Angela was happy to continue her life as a suburban mom and housewife in the middle-class town of Farmingdale on Long Island and spend summer vacations in Ireland with her mother, brother and sisters.

Vincent was a true-blue NYPD veteran. He started his career as a housing cop on bike patrol in Queens, and he eventually worked his way up the ladder to become a member of the elite Emergency Service Unit's Squad 3 in the Bronx.

His colleagues loved him. "He was short, so he took a lot of short hits," Detective Eddie Foley, who trained Danz in the ESU, said. "We taped a measuring chart by the door to measure his growth spurts over the years, like you do for kids."

Like many cops who accumulate large amounts of overtime, he would have been eligible to retire from the force in his late forties. He had plans for the future, too. He had returned to engineering school to learn how to operate a crane, as he enjoyed construction-related work, and he had hoped to work as a crane operator full-time after his retirement.

Being the spouse of a NYPD officer can often bring about tense times as it's one of the most dangerous jobs in the world. Angela remembers plenty of anxious moments.

"In the beginning when he was on the beat I was never really concerned about him," she says. "But when he was on nights I never fully slept. I did feel somewhat safer when he joined Emergency Services. They go into controlled situations and have back-up. Those men would give their lives for one another. I always believed that God was watching over him and he was always doing okay."

That was certainly the case up until 11 September. His safety would have been assured on that fateful day also, if he hadn't switched his scheduled 4 p.m. to midnight shift to one early in the morning, so that he could attend an evening class.

After Angela sent her two eldest girls off to school that morning, she met her neighbours for their customary walk around their community. One of her friends delivered the news that a plane had crashed into the World Trade Center. When the second aircraft attacked the remaining tower, Angela knew that the crashes were no accident and that her husband would be in the thick of things in his role as an Emergency Services officer.

"I had a bad feeling in the pit of my stomach," she remembers about the immediate hours after the attacks. "I rang my sister-in-law and said, trying to keep a brave face, 'Jesus, I'm not going to see Vincent for days, talk about overtime.'"

A check of her answering machine showed a flashing light. It was a call Angela Danz will regret missing for the rest of her life. At 9.50 a.m., Vincent Danz phoned to check in with his wife and assure her that he was fine despite the horrors unfolding all around him.

"The message said, 'Hi, hon, I'm just calling to say I'm okay. There were a lot of hurt people here. Please pray for them and pray for me. I love you. I'll see you when I get home.'"

It was the last time Angela Danz would hear from her husband. Vincent Danz died in tower one, trying to evacuate the building before it tumbled into a mass of dust at 10.29 a.m. Never did she think the light of her life, the man who made her transition from Ireland to America so easy, would not be coming home again. The last message from Vincent was recorded over, and in a way Angela was relieved that she wouldn't have her husband's haunting words to remind her of the tragedy.

"I probably would torture myself listening to that last message over and over. The FBI is trying to find it; but if they don't, I'm not meant to have it."

In the trying days immediately after the terrorist strikes, Angela surprised herself with her resilience. She felt she needed to stay strong for the sake of her girls, who now were forced to face life without the love and affection of their beloved father.

"I have three children. When you have children, you have to function. You can't sit in the corner with a bottle of whiskey. You have to live. With children, life is simple. Life is uncomplicated; you can't complicate it," she said.

"Everybody else gets to go home, gets to go to bed with their loved one. I never will again," Angela told the *Irish Voice* newspaper. "That's very difficult for me. Vincent was the centre of my world. My husband was my whole world. We were very close. We were each other's best friend."

Losing her spouse so suddenly and unexpectedly was a shock to Angela's system. The two were, in Angela's words, inseparable.

Vincent was a doting father by all accounts. At his memorial in October, he was remembered as an officer who always liked to leave the second his shift ended so he could rush home to his girls. "He adored his wife and kids," his fellow police officer, Eddie Foley, told the New York *Daily News*. "That's all he ever talked about." Danz and his daughters were often spotted around the neighbourhood on their bikes; watching cartoons and children's programmes on the Nickelodeon station was also a favourite pastime.

"For him his family came before anything else," Angela proudly says. "He was an outstanding father. He always made time for his family."

The funeral mass for Vincent Danz took place on 5 October at St Kilian's Church in Farmingdale. Danz was the first of the 27 NYPD officers who died on 11 September to be memorialised, and more than 2,000 family members, friends and colleagues paid their last respects. A heartbreaking picture of eight-year-old Winifred Danz appeared in all the New York papers the next day; the little red-headed girl was awash in tears as she held her father's police hat. Winifred also summoned the courage to read from Ecclesiastes during the mass, and Angela O'Reilly Danz touchingly eulogised her late husband.

Mayor Rudy Giuliani and his police commissioner Bernard Kerik made the trip to Long Island from Manhattan for the mass. The mayor said that Danz "laid down his life for people who weren't his friends, people he didn't know, people he'd never get to meet". Kerik was equally effusive in his words of praise. "To his colleagues in the NYPD, Vincent Danz is a hero who will never be forgotten."

Angela will never, ever forget the man who stole her heart when she first arrived in the States. But the task of raising three children without her husband in a land that's also 3,000 miles away from her immediate family was just too much for her to deal with. Angela quickly made plans to return to Ireland with her girls, and they made their move in December 2001, just in time for the loneliest Christmas of their lives.

"This country has been very good to me, but I will not miss it enough to stay," she told the *Irish Voice* before her departure. Her husband's death brought Angela full circle back to Dundrum, and now she's trying to pick up the pieces and create a stable environment for her fatherless children as best she can.

During a conversation with Angela in February, she said she was pleased with her decision to leave New York, but the move made the realisation of what happened to Vincent all the more real and difficult to cope with. Having her parents so close by has helped her and the girls immensely, she said.

She returned and moved right in with her mother and father, and then she set about finding a permanent home of her own. By Easter she was hoping to move into a house across the road from her brother that was in the process of being renovated.

Angela admits she's taking life one day at a time, with all her energies concentrated on the well-being of her girls as they settle into a new environment.

"I don't think about myself," she says. "I guess I keep myself busy so that I won't. But I'm no better now than I was in New York. The reality has sunk in, almost. Being here it is more real, more raw. If I was given the opportunity, I'd stay in bed three out of the seven days."

Her New Yorker girls are naturally finding the adjustment to life in Ireland strange, missing the friends and cousins they had on Long Island. Winifred and Emily are enrolled in non-denominational schools in Dundrum, as they had participated in the similar public schooling system in Farmingdale. Their mother drives the girls there in the morning, and a bus brings them back home after class is over.

"I wanted to keep that aspect constant," Angela says. "It's been hard, but the girls are doing well. They are making friends and doing normal things. I've signed them up for speech and drama. They had always been here on vacation so it's not as if suddenly they were hearing strange accents. But it is a bit strange."

Still, Angela is determined to give her children as normal an upbringing as possible, given the daunting circumstances. She was planning a one-year birthday party for baby Abigail in March, with cake and toys and all the trimmings, and was intent on helping to immerse her two eldest girls in Irish life as much as she could.

Vincent's daughters miss him, Angela says. "It's terrible for them. And the saddest thing is that Abigail will never know her father. She will only know him through me. I will tell her about him, I will show her her father. I have a lot of photographs. I will tell my girls that their father was a living, breathing hero."

Though there will be tough times ahead, Angela O'Reilly Danz is where she wants to be, post-11 September, that is. She feels she made the right move, and now it's time to get on with the task of living. But it won't be easy.

"I felt it was too much to be in New York," she says. "Here we are surrounded by family, but Vincent was the main event there. Now, he is not. It's strange, but it hit me all of a sudden this time that whereas I used to come here on vacation I would go back. Now I'm not on vacation any more."

CHAPTER EIGHTEEN

THE FIRE ON THE FRONTLINE

G ROWING UP IN South Armagh presented its own sometimes difficult challenges to 41-year-old Gerry Grant, a New York City court officer who specialises in first aid assistance. Though he hadn't been directly affected by the violence there, he and his wife Rita had seen their fair share of it.

But never did they think their lives in New York would be affected by, of all things, terrorist-related violence. That was something they left behind when they came to the US more than 20 years ago. Or so they thought.

In the middle of the mayhem on 11 September, a strange thought came to Gerry Grant's mind. "I said to myself, 'I survived 25 years in the North and I'm going to die at the hands of terrorists.' But I managed not to give in."

Grant's day had started out routinely enough. He left his suburban home in Rockland County after 6 a.m.; he took the train to Hoboken and transferred to the New Jersey PATH train that took him to the World Trade Center at 8 a.m. From there it was just a block and a half to 60 Center Street, where he was going to be recertified as the first aid responder. Grant was at the Officers' Academy that morning to have his first aid qualifications updated.

At 8.47 he felt the building shake. At first he thought it was the air-conditioning malfunctioning, but then the door burst open and a member of the staff told them that a plane had hit the World Trade Center. The first thought he had was the story of a plane crashing into the Empire State Building many years before.

Assembling with the other court officers, Grant was about to leave for the disaster site when the second plane hit. Grant and his fellow officers immediately sprang into action.

"We all got split up, and I ended up with two FBI agents and two NYPD officers," he recalls. "We were assigned to evacuating the buildings. I remember getting there and seeing this chunk of the plane on the ground. I picked it up to put it out of the way. It was just lying in the street.

"People were running everywhere. They were running away as we were running in. The buildings were burning, and there were pieces of the buildings falling everywhere. People were running northwards trying to get away, and there was word on the street that there were more planes heading to New York."

The pandemonium, he says, was simply unimaginable. But it never struck him that the buildings might actually collapse. "That didn't enter my mind," he says.

The force of the crashing debris was such that thousands of people who were attempting to escape the inferno were thrown to the ground, many never to rise again. The air was thick with smoke and dust, and visibility was next to zero. "We picked people up and told them to go north."

In the middle of his evacuation efforts, he came across two women standing stock-still on the street, holding on to each other. Their faces told the story: they were literally paralysed with fear. Grant took care of them and escorted them out of the danger zone. "Go north," he told them.

Now he knew that the second tower was likely to come down, too. Grant and his colleagues commenced intense evacuation efforts at the still-standing tower. "We were in the second wave of rescuers going in. We ended up in front of the second building," he says. "It became imperative that the building be evacuated. I heard afterwards that there were warnings on the street to clear the streets because the second building was coming down. We did not get that warning."

Grant noticed a fireman sitting on the ground, too exhausted to move. Then the second building began coming down. "The fireman had his oxygen mask and knew he could not move, so he told me to go." Grant slapped the mask on and started to run. (Miraculously, the fireman who saved his life also survived the crash.)

Grant was just 25 yards or so away when the 1,350-feet-tall building disintegrated. He remembers running through a sea of virtual blackness and being barely able to breathe. "I thought we were all going down. It was like an earth-quake at first," he says. "Then when the buildings went down, you couldn't call out for help because the dust would kill you."

A vital lifeline came when he grabbed a bottle of water from a nearby pharmacy. He pulled the mask off and, using his first-aid training, removed his shirt, soaked it with the water and then held it to his mouth to help him breathe.

"I know I was in that darkness for three minutes. But 30 seconds in and I could not breathe," he says. "I kept dous-ing the shirt, but then I ran out of water, and I was taking the shortest of breaths. By now I could hardly open my eyes."

At this stage Grant says he was fearful for his life, and thoughts of his wife and three young sons raced through his head.

Confused, he had no idea which way was out. Then an odd stroke of luck came his way. He tripped over an object that turned out to be a fire hose. He grasped it and followed its lead, and eventually it brought him to a fire truck. Its dimly shining red lights, which Grant could barely make out, were a sight for sore eyes.

"Within two yards of the truck the firemen inside saw me and yanked me inside," Grant says. They gave him medical treatment and flushed his eyes out with solution. He also coughed up a chunk of concrete the size of a marble.

"My eyes weren't right for three days after," he offers. "It helped flushing them, but there was so much dust under my eyelids, just closing them made them worse."

Safe for the time being in the truck, Grant and his res-cuers waited until some sort of visibility returned, still shocked at the earth-shattering events around them. Then they recommenced their rescue efforts.

It was bedlam when Grant returned. People were all over the streets, not knowing what to do or where to turn. There were people screaming, others crying. The dust cloud still hung over everything. He tried as best as he could to ensure the safety of some people.

Grant's eyes filled once again and he could barely see, but he refused EMS offers of assistance and continued to seek out the injured. There was no time for having his eyes treated, he felt, when thousands were mortally wounded.

"My emotions were running high that day," he remembers. "You know, had I been on the other side of the block I would not be here, given the way the building came down. Nobody expected this to happen, so it was difficult to be prepared and organised. I have never really thought about dying. Had I been on the other side, had the building fallen on my side, had I fallen and been unable to get up – it doesn't bear thinking about."

Grant lasted another two hours or so before his eyes completely gave up. He returned to his command centre at the courthouse, took a shower – he remembers lingering in the hot water for an hour – and called home.

Rita Grant wasn't at all worried about her husband because she assumed he was stationed in Queens at the other academy for the day. When he informed her that he was on duty in Manhattan, she naturally panicked; but he didn't tell her the extent of how involved he was in the rescue efforts.

Grant's two school-aged sons, Conor, 9, and Ryan, 7, were anxious about their father's safety, so much so that he had to place a phone call to their school to ease their fears. They didn't rest easy until they saw their father in the flesh. His three-year-old son Barry was, mercifully, too young to understand.

Three court officers were killed that day, including Captain Harry Thompson, who went down with Grant to the disaster site, so Gerry Grant recognises how fortunate he is to be alive.

Not alone did he personally survive the 11 September

attacks, he also is credited with helping save the lives of a countless number of others. But he's not interested in credit. As far as Gerry Grant is concerned, he says he was "just doing my job".

CHAPTER NINETEEN

BIN LADEN'S PURSUER

TOM DURKAN FROM Newark, New Jersey, remembers the time in 1996 that top FBI man John O'Neill called him up and asked for some of the best seats on the viewing stand for the St Patrick's Day parade in New York. Durkan, 78, who was also John Cardinal O'Connor's personal lawyer, had no problem obliging O'Neill.

That same year O'Neill also attended the cardinal's annual St Patrick's event after the parade itself. Gerry Adams, leader of Sinn Féin, was there, and though the two men did not meet, O'Neill subsequently followed Adams' career with great interest.

What happened next with the cardinal was not untypical where O'Neill was concerned. He and O'Connor became fast friends. As a former military chaplain, O'Connor had enormous time for the man who had the job of preventing terror attacks in New York. The men spoke at least two or three times a week and often went to dinner. O'Connor even gave him a set of archdiocesan cuff links, a gift reserved for special friends.

O'Neill would take leave on St Patrick's Day and was always an honoured guest of the cardinal at subsequent parades. One photograph showed him standing close to the cardinal on the cathedral steps as O'Connor reviewed the parade. One of the last gifts that O'Connor got before his final illness was a book from O'Neill presented at a retirement dinner for a mutual friend, a secret service officer.

O'Neill was also very friendly with Pat Byrne, the Irish garda commissioner, and looked forward to showing him around "his"city, New York, whenever he arrived over.

O'Neill certainly knew all the hangouts. "There wasn't an Irish pub on Second or Third Avenue that he didn't know people in," says Durkan. "Two particular favourites were Joyce's and the Green Derby."

Even though he liked a good time, O'Neill never neglected the day job. "It was business from morning to night," remembers Durkan, "even when we went to dinner."

Durkan estimated that O'Neill would spend about 15 per cent of the time eating and talking and the rest "would be him making calls, or leaving dinner to take calls on his cell phone.

"He was consumed to a fault with the obligation imposed upon him as special agent in charge of foreign counter-intelligence. I never met anyone with more dedication to an undertaking, nor did I know anyone who was more committed to fulfilling his responsibilities." Durkan also met many associates of O'Neill's and says that "all of them, without exception, held him in the highest esteem".

Work was his overwhelming obsession. "The FBI was like a mistress," said one agent. Once Durkan, O'Neill and another top FBI official had planned a golfing trip to Ireland, but it got postponed because O'Neill had to deal with an emergency situation. Durkan found that happened a lot with O'Neill; he always seemed concerned that something big was brewing against New York. As the special agent in charge, O'Neill carried a huge responsibility.

In some of their dinner conversations, Durkan remembers that the name Osama bin Laden came up, though only in a general sense. Durkan says that O'Neill felt that certain actions should have been undertaken against bin Laden, that he was being underestimated, and that he hoped that some plans would be implemented shortly. His hopes were in vain.

"What he did tell me about him was that he was a very definite threat and that a lot more attention had to be paid to the man. He was always convinced that there would be a repeat effort at the World Trade Center."

Who knows how it would have turned out if he had been listened to. Shortly after 11 September a book entitled *Bin Laden, the Hidden Truth* was published in Paris. Authors Jean Charles Brisard, a French intelligence expert, and Guillaume Dasqie, the editor of *Intelligence Online*, dedicated their book to John O'Neill, the Irish American FBI agent who, they categorically stated, was the only man who had ever come close to cracking the bin Laden network before 11 September.

O'Neill, the grandson of Irish immigrants who settled in Atlantic City, New Jersey, had been an FBI nut all his life. In his parents' third-floor walk-up, not far from the crashing Atlantic Ocean and the famous boardwalk, O'Neill became fascinated by the FBI series with Efrem Zimbalist on television. From an early age he felt his life was set. A career in the FBI was all that was important.

His career would see him reach close to the very top of the famed agency. Among the terrorist operations that he investigated were the bombing of the USS *Cole* in 2000 in Yemen Harbour, the 1998 bombing of US embassies in Kenya and Tanzania and the 1993 World Trade Center bombing. He played a key role in the arrest and conviction of the mastermind of that bombing, Ramzi Yousef.

In 1993, after the first World Trade Center bombing, John O'Neill told colleagues that Osama bin Laden, an obscure Saudi Arabian multimillionaire who had been linked by wiretaps to the conspirators, not Ramzi Yousef, was at the centre of the terrorist conspiracy against America.

"He said, 'We've got to get that guy. He's building a network. Everything leads back to him,' remembers Richard Clarke, the national coordinator for counter-terrorism in the first Bush White House, speaking in an interview with *New Yorker* magazine.

Bin Laden had first come to the attention of the counter-terrorism experts after the 1993 explosion that killed six. His name was spotted on a list of major donors to a charity linked to the bombing, and he was referred to as "the sheik" in several wiretapped conversations.

For the next eight years John O'Neill became the most

dedicated enemy of bin Laden, seeking to track him all over
the Middle East and beyond. As he rose in the FBI ranks, he
told anyone who would listen that America was the real
target of bin Laden and his al-Qaeda network. Authorities,
however, were much more fixated on the Iraqi or North
Korean threat and the idea of a rogue nation firing missiles
at the United States.

O'Neill knew, however, that the notion of any nation
challenging the United States to a conventional war was
becoming absurd. American military superiority was so great
that any country that threatened it would be obliterated. He
thought it much more likely that the new wars would be
against terrorist cells able to penetrate the United States
through its relatively open borders.

Unfortunately, very few paid any attention. Many considered him a nuisance with his continued insistence on the
importance of bin Laden and terrorism. The notion of a
major terrorist attack on United States territory simply had
very little traction.

O'Neill continued on his quest, however, as he rose
through the ranks, seeking information all over the world,
wheeling and dealing with many sources, cajoling here,
praising there, threatening somewhere else.

Kevin Giblin, a senior FBI counter-terrorism agent,
recalled him as "similar to an old Irish ward boss . . . you
collect friendships and debts and obligations because you
never know when you are going to need them."

When he made top rank at the FBI, O'Neill even joined
forces with the CIA, although the two organisations are
notoriously prickly about their own turf, in order to try and
get bin Laden. He helped create a new CIA station, with the
code name Alex, in the Middle East which had as its sole
purpose tracking down Osama bin Laden.

In June 1997 in a speech in Chicago, O'Neill warned,
"Almost all the [terrorist] groups today, if they chose to,
have the ability to strike us here in the United States." Again
his prophetic words were essentially ignored. He had his
share of enemies in the bureau and in the intelligence community, partly due to his indiscreet lifestyle.

John O'Neill, darkly handsome, with slicked-back hair and with a well-deserved reputation for wanting the best things in life, whether it was beautiful women, high society or access at the highest levels, was hardly a typical FBI agent, where anonymity is treasured and ostentation shunned. He favoured expensive cigars and high-end Scotch. He carried an automatic pistol strapped to his ankle. He dressed to kill and, when in New York, often hung out at Elaine's, one of the most exclusive night spots in the city. There he would meet his many important friends. "John O'Neill had this city wired," said one agent who knew him well.

Once he was pictured with Robert De Niro aboard Tommy Mottolla and Mariah Carey's yacht. In his office there were copies of French impressionist paintings rather than family photographs. His office was always full of fresh flowers. He was certainly not a product of the straightlaced FBI of the J. Edgar Hoover era.

His love life was tangled. He had married his high school sweetheart, Christine, in 1971 and was only 20 when their son John Junior was born. A daughter, Carol, was born later. His wife, however, did not join him when he moved to Chicago to become chief of the Bureau there in 1991.

After arriving in the Windy City, he soon began squiring Valerie James, a fashion director. When he transferred to Washington headquarters, he began a relationship with Anna Di Battista, a travel agent. When he moved to New York, both women, unaware of the other's existence, moved with him. Somehow he also kept the relationship with his first wife and family going. For his friends and acquaintances, however, it became increasingly puzzling. His Washington friends only knew his relationship with Anna, his Chicago buddies knew Valerie, while some of his old friends knew only his wife Christine.

As a result of O'Neill's success in nailing many of the principals of the first World Trade Center bombing, he was promoted to counter-terrorism chief of the FBI in Washington in 1995. There he became an expert on and one of the FBI's most important operators against Islamic fundamentalist terrorism.

In Washington O'Neill was part of a small team working around the clock on Islamic terrorism, all reporting to Richard Clarke. The immediate circle, known as the Counter-Terrorism Security Group, was drawn from the FBI, the CIA, the National Security Council, the Defence Department, the Justice Department and the State Department. They met once a week in the White House Situation Room. In several briefings, O'Neill warned that the takeover by the Taliban of Afghanistan was the most serious problem threatening American security in decades.

O'Neill believed that after the demise of the Cold War, America had been lulled into a false sense of security and that future wars would not be fought along conventional lines where countries attacked each other. Instead he pushed for a new approach which would seek to link all the terrorist incidents taking place, especially in the Middle East, in the belief that they were all planned by the one central agency. He was opposed by many of his colleagues, who believed he was giving bin Laden and his ilk far too much credit. They argued that Middle East terrorists would never have the wherewithal to attack the United States on home soil.

In the spring of 1996, O'Neill's theory received a major fillip when Jamal Ahmed al-Fadl, who had worked for al-Qaeda, turned himself in at the American Embassy in Eritrea. Fadl described for the first time the huge network that bin Laden controlled, his determination to attack America and his ambition to secure nuclear weapons. Despite the overwhelming evidence, the State Department refused to list al-Qaeda as a terrorist organisation.

On June 25 of the same year, al-Qaeda proved what they were capable of. They exploded a bomb at a military housing complex in Saudi Arabia where American troops were billeted. Nineteen were killed and 500 were injured. O'Neill was in charge of the investigation. The bomb used was the largest the agency had ever investigated.

O'Neill believed that the Saudis hindered the investigation and that they were unreliable allies because of their fears that bin Laden would turn on them. Global concerns at the

Clinton White House meant that such concerns were under-played.

Soon after he moved to New York, O'Neill created a spe-cial al-Qaeda desk. Shortly after, the American embassies in Kenya and Tanzania were bombed with heavy casualties, killing 224 people. As soon as the bombings took place, O'Neill tagged bin Laden as the prime suspect. Five defen-dants were arrested and convicted. The US prosecutor who secured the convictions stated that "John O'Neill created the template for successful investigations of international terror-ism around the world."

O'Neill also realised that many of the al-Qaeda opera-tives were active in the US. Ironically, under strict domestic spying laws, he was less able to keep track of them than if they had been living abroad.

He was deeply concerned about al-Qaeda actions during the Millennium celebrations. Then on 14 December 1999, a border guard in Washington State stopped a car driven by an Algerian, Ahmed Ressam, who ran off but who was later apprehended. In the trunk of the car were the ingredients to make a bomb bigger than the one that killed 168 people at Oklahoma City.

O'Neill followed up the valuable leads yielded by Ressam under interrogation. He arrested one of the ring-leaders, Abdel Meskini, in Brooklyn after a month-long stake-out. Then on New Year's Eve, O'Neill and colleague Joseph Dunne, a senior New York City police officer, went to witness the celebrations in Times Square in fear that al-Qaeda might strike. A jubilant O'Neill called friends after midnight to tell them that all was well.

Despite his successes, however, O'Neill was a target of major FBI infighting. He had many detractors in Washing-ton, both for his lifestyle and his take-no-prisoners attitude to those he disagreed with. He was passed over for the top job in New York in early 2000, and he knew his days as head of the Joint Terrorism Task Force were limited. His major protector, FBI Director Louis Freeh, was set to retire in June 2001.

Then came a bizzare incident at an FBI conference in

Orlando, Florida. O'Neill left a top-secret document in a briefcase that went missing after he left a meeting to take a call. Although the police recovered it a few hours later, the briefcase had been opened and some of the contents, though none of the classified material, stolen. The Justice Department ordered an immediate enquiry.

On 12 October 2000, al-Qaeda struck again, this time in Yemen, when a small boat carrying suicide bombers crashed into a US destroyer, the USS *Cole*. Seventeen American sailors died and 39 others were seriously wounded. O'Neill was put in charge of the investigation. He found himself in immediate conflict with the US ambassador, Barbara Bodine, who saw her job as protecting the relationship with the Yemeni government, which she had cultivated.

When O'Neill suggested that he and some agents go door to door to question locals, she told him incredulously, "You want a bunch of 6 foot 2 Irish Americans to go door to door. How many of your guys speak Arabic?" O'Neill had to admit there were very few. There were several other stand-offs, and O'Neill eventually returned home defeated, feeling that his own government had not supported him. John "had a pretty good Irish temper", said one senior government official after the incident.

He was on the cusp of retirement, with only one job that interested him: that of overall head of counter-terrorism in the second Bush administration. However, his stormy record with the FBI, as well as the Justice Department investigation into the briefcase incident, meant he would almost certainly be passed over if he tried for it, even though the current occupant recommended him.

At age 49, with an exacting lifestyle to support, he decided to leave the bureau and retire. A job in the private sector had caught his eye, that of chief of security at the World Trade Center in downtown Manhattan, paying $300,000, a fortune for him and three times his current salary. He was set to start on 1 September 2001.

"We talked about it a lot," remembers Tom Durkan. "I was giving him ring instructions on the new job. He was coming from a regimented, disciplined background and going into a business environment. I knew it was going to be a great change for him."

Friends say the last few weeks after he left the bureau were happy ones, finally free of all the infighting. On Monday, 10 September, John O'Neill, as was his wont, was out on the town, dropping in at Elaine's and also going to the China Club, a midtown hotspot. His girlfriend Valerie waited up until 2.30 when he finally came in. The following morning he dropped her off at an appointment at 8.15 and went on down to his office on the 34th floor of the World Trade Center.

When the planes hit, John O'Neill's son, John Junior, on a train to New York from New Jersey, saw the massive plumes of smoke over the World Trade Center. He called his father who told him he was okay and was on his way outside to assess the damage. At 9.17, O'Neill's girlfriend Valerie received a call telling her he was okay. His other girlfriend, Anna Di Battista, who was on her way to Philadelphia on business, received yet another call from O'Neill. She knew from the tone of his voice that he was going to go back to save people.

Tom Durkan's son, Tom Junior, also talked to O'Neill soon after the attacks. He was fine, he told him, and was in a courtyard between the two World Trade Center towers.

The last person to see him was Wesley Wong, an FBI agent who arrived at the crime scene soon after and reported that O'Neill had headed back into the north tower after briefly speaking to him. He was never seen alive again.

At his funeral in St Nicholas of Tolentine Church in Atlantic City, where he had once been an altar boy, the skirl of the Irish bagpipers brought tears to the eyes of many of the 1,000 people or so in the congregation. Even Louis Freeh, by then former FBI chief, who had not cried since the bombings, found himself in tears. John O'Neill's widow was the chief mourner.

Tom Durkan gave a eulogy, and it still pains him to remember the events of that day. "You know, I can't remember what I said," he says now. "It was too painful for me."

Of the over 3,000 lives that the 11 September terrorist attacks took, John O'Neill's death in particular must have given considerable satisfaction to Osama bin Laden, if he became aware of it. O'Neill had had the Saudi terrorist in his sights for many years, but due to bureaucratic ineptitude and carelessness, bin Laden had always slipped away. Now he had killed his former nemesis, John O'Neill, who had once boasted "I am the FBI" to a colleague. With his retirement and subsequent death, they had lost their most valuable asset, the one man who might have stopped 11 September if given a free rein.

CHAPTER TWENTY

DWYER'S STORY

J UST A FEW minutes after a friend had alerted Jim Dwyer, 44, Pulitzer Prize winning writer for *The New York Times*, to the incredible events unfolding at the World Trade Center, he was settling down in his Washington Heights apartment in upper Manhattan to cover the biggest story of his life.

In a quiet moment between his frantically dialling his sources, the phone rang.

"It was the friend of a friend from Chicago, calling to say that two of the trapped victims were anxious to speak with someone, and that someone was me."

Dwyer, one of the most wired men in New York City, was also famous for his definitive book on the World Trade Center bombing in 1993, entitled *Two Seconds Under the World*. If anyone could help someone trapped in that building, it was he.

He picked up the phone and dialled the number. Patricia Puma answered the phone on the 86th floor of the north tower, where she and her boss, Jim Gartenberg, of the real estate firm Julian J. Studley, were trapped. Puma, 34, an administrator with the company, told him that a collapsed wall had crushed one of the stairwells and made it impassable; the other was still being showered with huge pieces of debris and was too dangerous to risk. Dwyer tried to patch in several emergency workers who could give solid advice, but the sheer scope of the tragedy meant that no one was available.

Dwyer was their only lifeline.

He started by telling them that it would take a very long time to rescue them, that in 1993 some victims had waited hours to be taken down. "I told them that as bad as it seemed people were going to come and get them, and they both seemed reassured to hear that."

He also assured them that the plane impact would not bring the towers down. He had spoken to the engineer who designed the trade towers after the first terrorist attack in 1993, who had told him that the towers were designed to absorb the impact of a fully loaded 707 jet, then the most powerful plane flying.

Gartenberg, 36, an associate director with the Julian J. Studley firm, which specialises in commercial real estate, then told him that smoke was beginning to filter into the rooms and that he was about to break the windows to get some air.

"I warned them that if you break the windows that draws the smoke, which was something they found out in 1993: that opening windows was a disaster. I told him to place wet towels under the cracks in the door, and I told them not to worry. Gartenberg seemed comforted that wetting the towels and covering cracks under the door made sense to him and allowed him to do something affirmative."

Gartenberg, Dwyer remembers, was anxious but rational. Only once, when he asked him how old he was, did Gartenberg allow the anxiety to spill over. "I'm 36, and I really want to be 37 soon," he told Dwyer.

Patricia Puma was increasingly scared about their situation, especially when the south tower went down after being struck by the plane. More and more her voice betrayed an impending dread at what now seemed likely to happen to them.

Dwyer kept the conversation focused on the immediate danger. He did not discuss their families, whether they would live or die, and they did not want to either. "We were not thinking about death. We wanted to talk about living," Dwyer recalls.

He was then called away by an urgent phone message.

When he called back for the last time, there was only a ring-ing phone, then an ominous silence. The two died when the tower collapsed, and to this day Dwyer finds it difficult to speak about the two brave souls he had so desperately tried to help save.

If they had been on the other side of the building on that floor, he says, the chances were that they would have been saved. Almost all of the employees of the New York State Taxation Office on that side were able to get out and come down safely, though a few perished. The stairwells on that side were mercifully free.

Throughout his conversation with the two, Dwyer knew also that a possible personal tragedy was unfolding for him. His daughter, Maura, was at Stuyvesant High, an elite school which was located only a stone's throw from Ground Zero. In addition, his wife Cathy worked near by at Pace University and on a normal day was certain to have travelled through the subway stop at the World Trade Center on her way to work.

The fact that she and Jim had voted that morning in the Democratic primary may well have saved her life. She was late leaving, and Dwyer knew that it was unlikely that she would have made it as far as the towers by 8.45 when the first bomb hit.

The most intense period of his life ended when his daughter was reported safe after the school was evacuated, his wife was also reported safe, and Gartenberg and Puma perished in the north tower.

But that was only the beginning of his day. Right after, Dwyer was desperately seeking a way to get down to his office at the *Times*. Eventually he set off in his car with his bicycle propped up in the back, ready to cycle whatever the distance was if automobile traffic was blocked.

To his surprise he made it easily down to his office in Times Square. Inside, in the-third floor, open-plan news-room, the most prestigious newspaper in the world was gird-ing up for the biggest story that reporters would ever cover.

The editor, Howell Raines, ensconced in his small private office at the front of the newsroom, was only one day on the

job after moving from that of editorial page editor. Editors
huddled in the front page conference room. Assignments
were being handed out all over the globe.

Dwyer himself, the son of Irish immigrants from Kerry
and Galway, was a relative newcomer who had joined the
paper from the *Daily News* a few months previously. He had
broken into journalism with a famous column in *Newsday*,
writing about everyday life on the New York subways. He
travelled up and down the system, day after day, reporting
what he saw. The impact was so great that a movie was made
of his columns, as was a bestselling book, and he was sought
by every major newspaper in America. A few years later
came the Pulitzer Prize. With his in-depth knowledge of the
World Trade Center and his links into every important
source of power in New York City, the story was made for
him. This story, however, was greater than anything he had
ever tackled. Yet what struck him was the calm at the eye of
the storm in *The New York Times* newsroom.

"The mayor was missing for a while, we heard of the
other planes crashing, and the rumours were running rife,"
he says. "We were venturing into an unknown world . . . we
had to go and cross the boundary line between plausible and
the worst corners of our imagination. Once that boundary is
crossed, all bets are off."

The paper, he remembers, had an amazingly well coor-
dinated approach to the story. "I was in charge of writing the
piece on the impact on New York outside of Ground Zero.
We had to get our stories in by 7 p.m."

It only became blindingly clear to him what had happened when Giuliani reappeared after his brush with death.
No fan of the mayor at the best of times, Dwyer suddenly
found a deep affection for him at the worst of times.

"It was only the mayor of New York who was able to
appear on television. President Bush was in flight and had not
been seen. Giuliani found poetry in the city's darkest moment;
he said the loss of life was more than any one of us could bear.

"It really hit me at that point. I was born on this island
and lived my whole life here. If you put me down anywhere
here, blindfolded me and spun me around until I was dizzy,

I could find my way home. I always thought this city was like the strings on a guitar, tightly wound, and that day almost broke it for all of us.

"The names started coming in of who was missing, people I knew all my life. Where I come from, sons and daughters of immigrants had gone right to Wall Street from high school and used their street smarts to get ahead. Wall Street was their wild west, their frontier, where armed with your wits and ambition you didn't need to have degrees.

"In addition I knew cops, firemen and rescue workers. I knew city officials and bureaucrats. I kept counting and counting the missing I knew. I expected everyone to be gone, and when they weren't I was swept with emotion. I felt a powerful surge of relief and gratitude.

"I don't know when I started crying. I was standing on the street corner near Ground Zero and a truck came along carrying body bags. I asked the driver how many he had. He showed me the manifest: 11,000 bags. I'm sure they've used many more than that with body parts and all, but just hearing it made me very emotional.

"I was on Irish radio on the Marian Finucane show. I had agreed to go on at an ungodly hour in the morning of 12 September New York time. My wife and two girls were sleeping in our bed when I came home. I was happy to have the girls there. I couldn't sleep, so I went on; and while I was waiting I heard a montage of voices, and one of them was Mary McAleese, the president, saying something like she was outraged.

"The voice that she spoke in was a very familiar one for the son of Irish immigrants, an Irish woman who knew her mind, who knew right from wrong, and it still gets me choked up to remember her. The thought that she was on our side in our darkest hour was very comforting to me."

With his extensive knowledge of the World Trade Center dating back to his book on the 1993 bombing, Dwyer knew that, despite the horrific number of casualties, the buildings had stood up longer than they had a right to.

"Fourteen thousand escaped from the buildings, compared to the Albert R. Murrah building in Oklahoma when a car bomb outside the building destroyed it and everyone in it."

The 1993 experience of the bombing helped save thousands of lives, he says. "There was much better lighting in the stairwells, the people were familiar with fire drills, they had good people to direct the evacuation. Those people with the bullhorns, those John and Jane bureaucrats, they saved thousands that day just by their directions, telling people not to look back, to get clear of the buildings as fast as they could. Most of those with the bullhorns died."

Right away Dwyer had no doubt who was responsible for the atrocity. "These people started in 1990 and killed Meir Kahane, a Jewish radical in New York. In 1993 they tried to blow up the World Trade Center, killing six and attempting to kill thousands. They blew up a barracks in Saudi Arabia, two American embassies in Africa, they bombed the USS *Cole*, and they were obviously prepared to go to any lengths. What we didn't know is that they had suicide bombers at their disposal.

"There wasn't a scintilla of doubt in my mind that we had to go after them with everything we had. We couldn't walk on our streets; our children couldn't go to school; we couldn't run our businesses; our friends, mothers, fathers, sisters were dying, being killed by lunatics.

"They were clever, diabolical people who pulled off four simultaneous hijackings and successfully attacked the biggest city in the world and Washington. I knew we had to go to war, that far more innocent people were going to die unless these people were stopped.

"I would grant to people who came after America hard on the Afghanistan military action the legitimacy of their critique, and I know there is much more that this country has to do. We have to spend billions now helping the people who were in these countries. I will grant no legitimacy to bin Laden or his ilk, however. The attempt to say he is on the leading edge of some human rights crusade is ridiculous to me."

When he looks back on those events, however, Dwyer will not remember the global impact or the horrific shock to the system, but rather the elemental reality he witnessed on that day.

"The buildings collapsed with incredible power – everyone talked about the storm of debris, the blackness of not being able to see. The remnants of the buildings, the dust, the tiny pieces of debris were travelling at 50 mph, lodging in people's mouths, lungs and choking many. That was the cold physics part, the laws of nature.

"Then almost in the next instant, people emerged from shops, from restaurants, from houses, from apartments, with water, with first aid, with care. It was life trying to restore its equilibrium, one spoonful at a time.

"The people were fighting back, not against bin Laden, but fighting against the pain, the hurt, the confusion they saw all around them. Lieutenant Roger Perino of the fire department told me that he had barely escaped with his life. As he was struggling north to get away, covered in soot and grime, people grabbed him, brought him into their apartment, washed him, gave him water to drink, washed his face.

"Silvano Tomasetti, the owner of Da Silvano restaurant, is a mile away from Ground Zero, and he saw all the refugees streaming past. He moved his tables out on to the streets and got his staff to make sandwiches, brought out water coolers, wireless phones, and he got a thousand people fed; and who knows how many were able to call loved ones.

"He is a wonderful Florentine. He took this Irish couple I know who came struggling up with a young baby who was hysterical. He sent them over to his apartment so they could rest and clean up and the baby could be calmed down and sleep.

"It's the truth about New York; it came out that day. It always was the truth, but this time we had to own up to it. What we saw at the end of the day was people who tried to destroy us with the laws of physics, but then the spirit answered. I was never so proud of my city."

CHAPTER TWENTY-ONE

A DISPATCH FROM GROUND ZERO

THE FIRST EXPLOSION came at 8.48 a.m., startling Conor O'Clery, international business editor of *The Irish Times*. O'Clery was in his Battery Park home office, looking out on the north tower of the World Trade Center.

O'Clery, 60, veteran of covering Russia, China, Washington and now Wall Street for his paper, was not aware he was suddenly about to cover the biggest story of his long newspaper career – that he was one of the very few journalists to witness it first hand.

It was a placid beautiful day; not a hint of a breeze. The Hudson River sparkled in the autumn sunshine, and from his apartment he could see the boats ferrying the commuters from New Jersey across to Wall Street.

In an ironic twist, just below O'Clery's building work was commencing on the Irish Famine Memorial, a famine-era cottage that was just beginning construction. As O'Clery says, he had come all the way to New York to enjoy a view of rural Ireland.

He had risen at 6.30 that morning and seen his wife, Zhana, off to work at 7.15. Their apartment, a penthouse suite on the 41st floor of a residential building, had unrivalled views of the twin towers and Wall Street to the east and the Hudson River, the Statue of Liberty and Ellis Island to the south and west. The northern tower was dead centre from his living room window, just a few hundred yards away. The south tower was partly obscured, but he could see the television and radio antennas which sprouted from its roof.

A house guest, Aoife Keane, daughter of an old colleague from Ireland and a 20-year-old college student, had been staying with the O'Clerys. The night before they had stood on the tiny balcony outside their apartment and gazed at the lights of the twin towers for some time. Aoife was excited on her first day in New York, and she was looking forward to going to the top of the towers, to the 107th-floor observation deck, the following day.

At 8.40, after perusing the *Financial Times* and *Wall Street Journal* and looking up his home site of *The Irish Times* on the web, O'Clery began working on a story on how the looming recession had already begun to affect the restaurant business in New York. Ten minutes later, hell broke loose.

"I heard a tremendous explosion, and I jumped up and looked out the window. I thought it had to do with some construction work that was going on near by. I immediately saw a gaping hole in the north tower of the World Trade Center and concluded it was an explosion inside the building. I hadn't heard any plane overhead, so I didn't immediately believe it was caused by an external impact."

(Down at the site of the Famine memorial, Brian Tully had seen the plane banking steeply coming off the Hudson River and realised with horror that it was accelerating as it approached the towers.)

By now O'Clery knew he was witnessing an incredible disaster. "The smoke was pouring out, and I estimated that the hole was at least ten storeys high. Flames could be seen beginning to encircle the upper floors of the building. I saw an office worker hanging out of a window and waving a white cloth, a shirt perhaps, trying to attract attention.

"I realised something terrible had happened. I called my wife to tell her I was okay, called my news desk to tell them a massive story was underway and called our Washington correspondent, Patrick Smyth, and told him to get down to New York as soon as possible.

"I also called RTÉ, the national radio station, in Ireland, and while I was waiting to go on the air I heard a news flash that a plane had hit the building."

O'Clery went into the spare bedroom to wake his guest. "I told her something dreadful had happened and to dress quickly. We went into the front room, and I was using my binoculars to focus on the man hanging out of the window when she said, 'Look, there's another plane.'

"I took down my binoculars, and at the last second I saw the second plane disappearing behind the north tower; and then from the other side I saw a massive explosion, and a huge ball of red and orange flames came shooting out. I saw debris raining down on the street, and I immediately knew anyone who was underneath would be killed instantly if it hit them.

"At this point I made the decision to go over to the World Trade Center, or as close as I could get. I'm a journalist after all, and we run towards the sound of gunfire. Now I realised that people were falling or jumping from the buildings.

"At this point the towers had not fallen. I never thought they would fall. I could see the dozens of fire engines jammed on to the West Side Highway, and my assumption was that the firemen would get the blaze under control from below. I remember thinking, why didn't a helicopter land on the roof to whisk people off? But I learnt later that the roof exits were closed, as evacuation procedures called for everyone to use the stairwells, which were blocked by the fire and falling debris. Nobody survived above the impact of the plane as a result.

"When I went down to the ground level and began walking to the twin towers, I met thousands fleeing from the fire, all very shocked. One woman was screaming, 'They're jumping; my God, they're jumping,' and I saw several people just like rag dolls falling from the sky. As I tried to get closer, a security guard held us back, very wisely as it turned out.

"I decided to return to my office, because I was aware that the entire place would be evacuated and I might never be able to get back there. In addition, I had my house guest,

a young woman from Ireland who was witnessing these horrific scenes.

"I met a woman crying in the foyer of my building that
her husband worked in the twin towers and she had not
heard from him. Others there were sobbing uncontrollably.

"I was just back when I saw the people gathered in Battery Park, a small grassy area, suddenly start to run for their
lives, and then I saw that the south tower was starting to collapse, slightly sideways at first. I saw it collapsing directly on
the fire engines and the firemen there who were still arriving.
I saw firemen disappear under massive chunks of buildings,
as big as houses as they fell. It was very distressing."

O'Clery shifted his gaze to the north tower and through
binoculars saw that the man waving the white cloth was still
there, desperately signalling from the window, hanging on
precariously by one hand with his body out over the abyss.

"I saw several more people had appeared in the upper
storeys and that some had commenced jumping. I wondered
again why there was no attempt to rescue them by helicopter,
as part of the building was still free of smoke."

O'Clery witnessed the immediate collapse of the second
tower, which had an even bigger impact than the first. He
saw the tower begin to shake slightly and saw two people
fall in quick succession. Then the tower simply imploded,
falling down on itself with an enormous crash. He remembers in the aftermath a massive cloud of dust and smoke like
a pea souper fog wafting towards his building. As it
approached, like an invisible hand, the wind blowing from
the west blew it back across the city just as it threatened to
engulf his building.

When it cleared O'Clery saw the most remarkable sight
of his life. "The area around the building was like a scene
from a nuclear winter. A white and grey toxic dust covered
everything in sight and seemed to be ankle deep. I saw mangled fire engines, cars on fire, people screaming and fleeing,
and I saw thousands of tons of rubble fall on Tobin Plaza
where open air concerts were often held and on the nearby
building which houses Borders' Book Stores.

"All the roadways and pavements, all the street cars, fire

engines, pavements, traffic lights, awning and police vehicles were covered with dust. The green park between my building and the towers, where the kids often play American football, had been transformed into a grey field as if covered with toxic snow; and then a deadly quiet fell as the enormity of what had just happened set in."

He saw choked and weeping people staggering up Greenwich Street and West Broadway, covered in white dust, some covering their eyes as if to ward off the horrific sights they had just seen.

He saw the ferries, which just moments earlier had shipped thousands across the Hudson from New Jersey to work in Wall Street, begin to return and fill up with people desperate to escape as the smoke drifted eastward to cover all of lower Manhattan. He saw immense scenes of destruction come into view, twisted piles of rubble and crushed vehicles, many of them fire and police trucks and cars.

Also among the rubble he saw bodies of those who had been desperately fleeing the scene but who never made it out alive. He saw no movement at all, the first inkling that very few would have survived the impact.

Suddenly the ominous sound of jet engines overhead caused instant panic on the streets below as another plane appeared. It was a military fighter jet which had set out to intercept the hijacked second plane, but which had arrived too late.

By now his building was being evacuated, but through sheer luck they never came knocking on his door, allowing him vital time to send his story across the airwaves to Ireland and to *The Irish Times*. "I was not aware of the incredible impact outside the US of the story," he says. "I only realised later that people all over the world had stopped what they were doing and watched television."

Back home in Ireland several of his children, relieved at first when they heard him on the radio, were suddenly fearful after he had not come on for some time after the collapse of the towers. "I had a great feeling of guilt, later, that I didn't call everybody and say I was okay, but the shock was so great."

O'Clery's wife, Zhana, had talked her way back into the building but was unable to come up to the 41st floor. With the electricity about to be cut off, O'Clery realised it was time to move to safety with Aoife.

As they left the building they became just two more members of a mass of humanity which was moving from downtown Manhattan north to the safety of the midtown area and beyond. The police were screaming, "Go north, go north."

What O'Clery remembers most were the many firemen he encountered on the walk. "They were stunned, moving along as if in slow motion. They knew they had lost hundreds of their comrades."

Along the way they stopped in a restaurant in Greenwich Village to eat a meal. None of them had had as much as a bite all day. In one of the more bizarre twists of an already incredible day, a fight broke out between the manager and a diner. Sitting at the table next to them was Hollywood star Helen Hunt. She ran out into the street when the fighting started. O'Clery remembers thinking, "This can't be happening."

Further along on the trek uptown he interviewed a doctor from the emergency room of St Vincent's, the closest hospital to the disaster, who told him he had been on duty all day waiting for injured, but that very few had come. Instead, the hospital had been besieged by relatives desperately seeking their loved ones. "I can only think it will be bad news for them all," the medico told him.

The atmosphere reminded O'Clery of a previous assignment in Djakarta, Indonesia. The Suharto government was about to fall, the city streets were full of looters and rioters, and the police and army had withdrawn. The same sense of shock was almost palpable in the air, as if people were refusing to believe what was happening.

"You knew something of great enormity had happened, and that the consequences would be very dramatic. I knew it was a day to change the world."

CHAPTER TWENTY-TWO

THE IRISH MOURN

UBLIN AND ALL cities and towns in Ireland ground to a halt in the wake of the 11 September tragedy. Ireland was alone among the countries of Europe in calling a National Day of Mourning, and the hundreds of thousands who attended services on the day gave ample evidence of the deep and lasting bonds between the US and Ireland.

Taoiseach Bertie Ahern asked that all businesses, colleges and school and entertainment outlets be closed on Friday the 14th. In addition, he requested that the public attend religious services on the Friday.

Even before the Day of Mourning, however, the public were lining up for hours outside the American Embassy in Dublin. There was a five-hour wait at one point to leave the messages of condolence and wreaths. *The Irish Times* headline ran "Thousands in Display of Grief at Embassy".

A New York Police Department baseball cap tied to the railings was a poignant reminder of what had been lost. People openly cried on each other's shoulders, and there were thousands of wreaths and personal messages left. Some children lit candles, while the scent of lilies, the flower of mourning, was overpowering.

The streets of Dublin were eerily deserted on the Day of Mourning. *The Irish Times* did not publish, and most businesses closed.

Across town at the Pro-Cathedral, thousands lined up outside, unable to gain entrance, as the taoiseach and the president led the prayers for the missing and the dead. Even though the outside public address system did not work, the crowd stayed.

The ecumenical Service of Remembrance was led by Cardinal Desmond Connell, the archbishop of Dublin, and Dr Walton Empey, Church of Ireland archbishop of Dublin. The Methodist, Presbyterian, Quaker, Russian Orthodox and Greek Orthodox churches were also represented.

Afterwards, when a group of Americans at the service stood on the steps and spontaneously began singing the "Star Spangled Banner", the words were taken up by many in the crowd. There was a special welcome for the members of the Dublin Fire Brigade, who received one of the loudest cheers of the day.

In her speech to mark the National Day of Mourning, President Mary McAleese said:

> We are shocked, sickened, grieving, disbe-
> lieving, outraged, frightened all at once. We
> are only beginning to hear the human stories,
> the unbearable reports of the final phone calls
> of love, of the heroism of so many, the loss of
> so many . . . Our first thoughts therefore are
> with the American people as they try to cope
> with the magnitude of what happened in
> their great country.
>
> We in Ireland face our own share of this
> tragedy. We have only to look at the photo-
> graph of the beautiful faces of Ruth Clifford
> McCourt and her gorgeous little girl Juliana
> to see with our own eyes the loss which Ire-
> land too has experienced.
>
> This National Day of Mourning is a very
> special opportunity for all of us . . . It sends
> a message across the Atlantic and indeed,
> around the globe that Ireland too is broken-
> hearted and grieving deeply at the uncon-
> scionable waste of life we have witnessed this
> week.

Over at the Clonskeagh Mosque in South Dublin, Imam Hussein Halawa was outspoken in his condemnation of what took place. "We strongly denounce and condemn any aggression, terrorism and killing perpetrated against the innocent people in any corner of the world," he said, "and in particular this horrible terrorist act which took place in America."

Meanwhile, the Islamic Foundation of Ireland, based in Dublin, reported receiving 90 abusive phone calls and six supportive ones after the 11 September incident. A spokesman told *The Irish Times*: "Our religion means peace; it means to submit to the word of God. I feel sad, angry and dismayed."

Across the island of Ireland, the grief and pain were evident everywhere. In Galway, over 5,000 people attended the remembrance mass at midday in the cathedral. Mary Robinson, the UN commissioner for human rights and former president of Ireland, attended the ceremony.

At Knock Shrine, one of Ireland's holiest places, over 6,000 attended a special memorial mass, while in Mullingar, over 2,500 attended an ecumenical ceremony at the Cathedral of Christ the King.

In Cork, over 1,000 attended a special service, and Bishop John Buckley stated, "There is little we can do except pray for those who lost loved ones in the disaster and express our solidarity with America, a country that has been good to Irish people all down the years."

In Belfast, thousands gathered in front of the City Hall for three minutes of silence, led by Lord Mayor Jim Rodgers and US Consul General Barbara Stephenson. In her remarks, the consul general said, "I have seen so many images this week that have told me about how much grief and despair there is . . . our countries today are united in grief." Meanwhile, in Derry, several thousand observed three minutes of silence at the Guildhall.

On radio and television the attacks utterly dominated coverage. Those Irish who narrowly escaped were interviewed at length, those dead or missing eulogised. Peter Kiley, a financial consultant from Tarbert, in Kerry, told how he was working on the 55th floor of the south tower when the plane hit. Unknown to him, his nephew Patrick Donovan, 21, a carpenter, was working 30 floors above him in the same building. Both Kiley and Donovan ignored calls to remain in the building and narrowly escaped with their lives.

Sean Lynskey from Galway was on the 37th floor in the south tower when the first plane hit. Once outside he looked up and saw a plane crashing into the second tower. "People really started panicking," he told *The Irish Times*. "It was total chaos."

At Shannon and Dublin Airports, thousands of passengers, many of them Americans, found their flights cancelled and had to make emergency arrangements to find accommodation. In Shannon, Father Tom O'Gorman, a local curate, made an announcement at evening mass that accommodation was urgently needed for the stranded passengers. There was an immediate response, and all the passengers were quickly given lodgings. "The community were wonderful and responded immediately," said Father O'Gorman.

Across the pages of the provincial papers, the heartbeat of rural Ireland, there were stories of survival, loss, grief and relief, many from Irish people in America who were near or part of the tragedy. In almost every newspaper, from Donegal to Kerry, there was an account of someone from the area, or of an Irish American with family ties to the region, who was caught up in the tragedy. The greatest American tragedy had hit very hard on Erin's shores, too.

As the *Mid Ulster Observer*, published in Omagh, site of the greatest atrocity of the Troubles, reported: "Over the centuries the United States and particularly New York has been a haven from oppression and famine for thousands upon thousands of Irish people. It reveals what all Irish people know to be true – that there are few families in Ireland without relatives in the United States."

The *Observer* told two stories of eyewitness accounts. Jimmy Loughran from Cookstown was working on the 34th floor of one of the towers when tragedy struck. He escaped within an inch of his life. Mark O'Loughlin from Maghera was in Washington, DC, when the attack on the Pentagon occurred but was fortunate enough to be far away from the building.

Sadly, Sean Canavan, whose parents were from Bally-gawley in County Tyrone, was especially remembered. A carpenter working on the 94th floor, Sean, an American cousin of famous Tyrone footballers Peter and Paschal, was reported missing.

The *Longford Leader* stated: "If anybody ever doubted the close connections between Ireland and America, then the past week should have left them in no doubt. Constant emigration, particularly from counties like Longford, Leitrim and Cavan, over the past 150 years has ensured that all over America, but particularly in the greater New York area, there are now thousands of people with connections to this part of Ireland. It was no wonder therefore that when tragedy struck New York and Washington on Tuesday, 11 September 2001, the people of Longford and adjoining counties felt almost as if the tragedy had occurred in their own county."

Sadly, that feeling was reinforced a couple of days after the New York disaster when word came through that some with close Longford connections had been among the victims and among those heroes who had helped with the rescue.

The *Longford News* told proudly of Joe Donavan, the New York firefighter who "has plans to renovate Newcastle House in Longford". Donovan, according to the *News*, "has been down on Ground Zero for the most part of the rescue effort and has done marvellous work."

The *Clare Champion* led with: "Clare Concern for Missing Irish". A New York firefighter who was missing, Bobby Linnane, was the son of the late Bridie Coughlan from Lissycassey, the report noted.

The *Wexford People* simply gave its entire front page over to a lonely picture of a deserted Wexford town on the day that Ireland stood still in memory of those that died or were lost in the tragedy.

In the *Westmeath Examiner* readers were told of an Athlone mother who had an anxious wait when she heard the news on the *Liveline* radio programme that two planes had hit the World Trade Center in New York.

"Nancy McManus was in her Baylough home when news broke of the disaster. Her immediate concern was for the safety of her son, 28-year-old David, who works with Oprah Winfrey's communications company close to Ground Zero in the city. Describing the ordeal, McManus said she immediately started calling her son David's number knowing that he would be travelling to his office at the time. 'It was like my world was coming to an end in those anxious moments,' she recalled. When eventually her son called, she described it as 'a wonderful feeling'."

In *The Kerryman* newspaper, two Kerry families were reported as facing the cruel reality that loved ones were among the thousands who perished in the World Trade Center. The Lynch family from Tralee was devastated to discover that their American cousin Michael was among the first firefighters to respond to the disaster call. The Williams family was mourning the loss of American relatives in the aftermath of the tragedy. Christina Williams, who emigrated from Tralee to the US, had two nephews working at the World Trade Center.

The *Connaught Telegraph* reported on the solidarity of Mayo firefighters with their US counterparts during the disaster: "In two hours last week, the firefighters from 12 towns in Mayo collected 8,000 signatures for a book of condolences."

In the *Western People*, Michael Commins reported: "Two New York firemen with Mayo connections were amongst those reported missing. They were firefighters Dennis McHugh and John Tierney whose fathers hail respectively from the Garrymore and Hollymount regions." According to the *People*, "10 months ago McHugh and his wife Una celebrated the birth of their twins. Tierney was a firefighter from Ladder 9 in Manhattan; he was last seen in the World Trade Center Tower One before it collapsed."

In the *Carlow People* it was reported that a Carlow family flew to New York in a bid to learn the fate of their daughter-in-law who was working in the World Trade Center at the time of the terrorist attack. "Frank Duggan went to New York with his two sons Colm and Alan as his daughter-in-law Jackie is classified as missing. Jackie was catering sales manager in the Windows of the World. New Yorker Jackie, who is married to Mitchell Duggan, was at work last Tuesday morning when the two terrorist planes crashed into the twin towers," the paper reported.

In the *Meath Chronicle* the front page told of "A Glimpse of Hell on Earth". According to the newspaper, many Meath exiles were caught up in the horror of the attacks in New York and Washington and were recounting their stories.

"A large number of Meath emigrants were in the immediate vicinity of the World Trade Center when the attacks began. Navan native Mary Hubrich, a member of the Marmion family that runs the popular Ludlow Street pub, works a 10-minute walk from the disaster area in Manhattan. Mary related how she had emerged from the subway on her way to work last week to hear that the two buildings had been hit. As she looked down Broadway, she saw the first collapsing. 'It was very frightening,' said Mary, who has worked in the US for eight years and is now employed in the investments sector."

Fellow Meath native Damian Creavin described seeing "a nuclear-like plume of smoke" when he emerged from the subway and looked down at the disaster area.

The bishop of Meath, Most Rev Dr Michael Smith, was one of the many Irish citizens awaiting confirmation of a relative's fate. His cousin, Patrick Aranyos, was missing and presumed dead in the ruins of the south tower. The paper also reported that a nephew of Tommy McHugh from Oldcastle, stockbroker Michael McHugh, was also thought to be among the thousands buried beneath the World Trade Center debris.

The *Nenagh Guardian* reported an outpouring of grief and shock in communities throughout North Tipperary for the loss of thousands of lives, including a Cappawhite, County Tipperary, native, Martin Coughlan, who had been doing contracting work on the 96th floor of the south tower. "Coughlan was buried on Tuesday in his adopted home of Bayside, Queens. He is survived by a wife and four daughters," the newspaper noted.

The *Sligo Champion* told the sad tale of Kieran Gorman, from Lavagh, who was first reported missing following the terrorist attack. According to the paper, Gorman worked with the Structure Tone construction company and was involved in work on the building at the time of the explosion. A former Sligo footballer, Gorman also played with the Sligo team in New York. A friend of his, Michael Burke, who lived in Tubbercurry for a number of years, went to the building after it fell to see if he could help out with the rescue efforts. "People here were still hoping and hoping," he said.

In an emotional interview with the *Champion*, the Gorman brothers spoke of Kieran's love of life, his passionate interest in Gaelic football, and his devotion to his wife, who was expecting the couple's third child in November.

Meanwhile, Irish Americans Sean McGovern and Damian Meehan, with strong local roots, were remembered in the *Donegal Democrat*.

The *Galway City Tribune* reported that there were many stories of Galway people who were lucky enough to survive narrow escapes. The *Munster Express* reported the extent of Irish support for Americans as it told of how the churches were packed to pray for America's dead. All across Ireland in every town and village, thoughts were with someone in America.

Meanwhile, on the IrishAbroad.com website, a book of condolences was set up and there were soon thousands of entries from Irish people all over the world.

"For the families whose calls go unanswered. We pray for you. Call someone you know and have not spoken to in some time, call them now," said John from Dublin.

"My deepest sympathy to all the victims, relatives and friends. Words are not adequate to express our feelings here in Ireland. God bless America. Our prayers are with you," wrote Mike Flynn in Ireland.

CHAPTER TWENTY-THREE

THE CONSTRUCTION MEN: A CLOSE BRUSH WITH DEATH

H E DRESSED THAT morning of 11 September in his usual work gear: T-shirt, jeans and work boots. His T-shirt read *"Ceol, Craic agus Ól"* on the back (Irish for music, fun and drink). On the front was the legend "Atlanta '96", where the Olympics had been held, and the logo for *Fadó*, a famous Irish bar in Atlanta, Georgia.

He was anxious to get to work. He had been unemployed for some weeks, up until the previous Sunday when he went to watch the All-Ireland hurling final in a Manhattan Irish bar. While there he had struck up a conversation with several fellow Irishmen who were looking for good construction men to work on a job at the World Trade Center south tower.

He was familiar with the location, having worked there for a brief period the previous February on another construction job. It would be light steel and concrete work. A key structural wall on the 23rd floor had to be reinforced, they told him, along with some other renovations.

He was happy because they were not asking for papers and said it would all be taken care of. There was nothing unusual about that in the world of Irish construction in New York, where many were illegal.

Because of his undocumented status, the lack of a need for working papers meant everything on this new job. A single man in his mid-thirties, he lived in constant fear of

being deported and stayed clear of all the usual Irish neighbourhoods, living outside New York in an area that had few
or no Irish. Because of previous legal problems in Ireland, he
was particularly intent on keeping a very low profile.

His first day at work, the Monday, had gone well,
although he had not known any of the crew he was working
with. Most were from the North, and he knew well enough
to keep to himself and ask no more questions than were nec-
essary. He was just happy to be employed again.

Tuesday dawned clear and sunny, "a nice old pleasant
morning", as he remembers it. He got the bus into the city
and connected with the subway line that would take him to
the World Trade Center. He arrived under the twin towers at
7.05 sharp.

Off the subway he saw two of his workmates from the
day before and walked along with them. He was reassured
to see them because he was afraid he would find it hard to
locate the exact security point he needed to pass.

As they walked, a group of other construction workers,
quite large in number, passed them. As they greeted each
other, he saw many Irish T-shirts and heard snippets of conversation about the hurling All-Ireland as they walked. He
knew they were working further up the building but did not
know where.

At the security check-in, they were all given badges and
allowed to proceed. They got in one of the massive elevators and pressed the 23rd floor. Just another day at work
beckoned.

By 7.30 that workday had begun. He was busy helping
to take various measurements. The man he was helping, a
northerner, was friendly and good-natured, and they were
getting along well.

Directly outside the window he noticed some scaffolding. He couldn't tell how far it went up the building, but it
cleared their floor and went upwards, he thought, to about
the 32nd floor. It was a completely different construction job,
which had nothing to do with them. He thought for a
moment it might belong to window washers.

They never heard the first plane crash into the building

beside them because the electric saws and construction implements were creating a racket. Their first inkling was when a security guard ran into the room with a look of sheer terror on his face. He screamed to them to get out of the building, that a plane had crashed into it.

"We didn't take him seriously at first," he remembers. "It seemed such a ridiculous thing to say."

They ran outside to the elevator bank, expecting to see all calm. What they saw instead was pandemonium. Hundreds of people were milling around in the hallway waiting for elevators that never came. Some were screaming, others were praying. All were searching frantically for an elevator or an exit. It was a scene out of hell, he remembers.

Quickly the Irishmen realised just how dangerous a situation they were in. They checked for the stairs exit but in the panic and confusion could not find it. Someone of their group shouted, "Scaffolding!" and they immediately ran back inside.

They clambered out the window and began their perilous descent, feeling the building groaning and straining under the weight of the plane attack. They smelt the foul, smoky air, and they knew they were in a desperate race for their lives.

He was the slowest of all, due to an old right-arm injury. It was his natural climbing arm, but he had to depend on his left, hauling himself down floor by floor using his left grip and his right elbow for balance. He wasn't sure he would make it.

Ahead of him his workmate, the man he had been measuring with, sensing he was in trouble, slowed down to encourage him. "He was looking out for me," he remembers now. "I will never forget him."

He made it to the ground just moments before the collapse. He believes he had got only about 30 yards clear when a massive rumbling sound signalled the crash of the building.

Down on the street, as the building came down, he saw everyone running for their lives, many bumping into each other and falling down. There were hundreds screaming. "It was pure hysteria, pandemonium."

He ran as fast as he could, but a choking dust began filling his lungs. He fell over some debris and had to haul himself back to his feet. He found it difficult to breathe and fell again.

The dust storm made day night, and he was blindly feeling his way in the blackness. Then something struck him on the back and he collapsed on the ground, hitting his head sharply, knocked out momentarily.

Two men saved his life, one in a uniform, though in the encircling gloom he couldn't tell if it was a police officer or a fireman. He regained consciousness as they dragged him clear; and then with one of his arms around each of their shoulders, they half-dragged, half-ran with him to safety. "They saved my life, and I will never get to thank them," he says now.

An ambulance was waiting to ferry the injured to the nearest hospital. He screamed when they tried to lie him on his back. He had a serious burn wound, and blood was pouring from his head. They told him his ribs were also broken and that he was incredibly lucky to have survived.

They brought him to St Vincent's Hospital, where they dressed the burn on his back and treated his broken ribs and his head wound. For the next several days, he had to lie on one side because the pain in his back was so brutal.

His only visitor was his workmate who had stayed behind to encourage him on the scaffolding. All the Irish he knew had got out alive, he told him, though several were injured. He knew nothing about the Irish on the other floors they had seen go into the building, but presumed they had got out.

Throughout Wednesday, Thursday and most of Friday he remained in the hospital, moved out of the emergency room on to a general ward as his condition improved. Then city officials arrived and began asking probing questions of every survivor about their background and their family ties.

Though the officials were trying to be helpful and to find out as much as they could about everyone so that families desperately seeking missing ones could be notified, he immediately panicked at the sight of the officials. He knew he was registered under a false name and that his status might well be revealed.

"I upped and left," he says. "I called for someone I knew to meet me, and we made it out of the hospital."

Still in need of treatment, he spent the next few days at the friend's house. Fortunately his friend's sister-in-law was a nurse and treated his burn wound. "Only for her I would have been in an awful state."

Though his physical wounds are now almost healed, the mental scars remain. "I am still shocked. I get awful flashbacks that I am falling and that I can't see in front of me. I wake up in a sweat and lie there with everything racing through my mind. I have had only one good night where I slept since it happened."

He is attending a psychiatrist who has told him he has post-traumatic stress disorder. He finds the doctor helpful and says he is finally able to open up with him and discuss the dreadful fears that haunt his nights. He hopes it will get better in the future, but when he closes his eyes he still sees the buildings fall and thousands of people panicking and screaming. "It will never leave me," he says, "but I have to learn to cope with it. I was lucky to get out alive."

"A GOOD DAY TO DIE"

For firemen and policemen, the events of 11 September, while gruesome (such as finding body parts), were in some ways similar to events they had likely experienced in their line of work many times. For men like Eamonn Carey, 30, being catapulted into hell was a very different and life-changing experience.

The Listowel, County Kerry, carpenter who came to America in 1993 was one of the first construction workers to the Ground Zero site. He spent the next few days as an unpaid volunteer desperately attempting to find survivors of the worst disaster in American history.

In the process, the soft-spoken Kerryman witnessed sights he will never forget and images that still haunt him even months after the tragic event. Sipping a pint in a Manhattan West Side bar, he still becomes visibly agitated and uneasy when remembering all that he went through.

Tuesday, 11 September, had started, as usual for him, at home in New Jersey, waiting for a construction job to start. A committed member and shop steward of Local 608, the most Irish union in New York City, Carey had worked for several weeks in the vicinity of the World Trade Center, ironically on the new Irish Famine Memorial in Battery Park, where he was foreman. On that day several of the union members were directed to the World Trade Center to work. He could easily have been one of men who went to work in the twin towers that day.

Instead, the first he heard was when his sister, Mairéad, a journalist in Ireland, called him to check if he was all right after she had watched the events unfold on television. Carey immediately knew many of his members would have been working in the towers, and he grabbed his construction gear and headed straight for the city.

Getting to Ground Zero was easier said than done. The bridges and tunnels entering Manhattan were all closed, as were all the major highways from New Jersey to the city, including the New Jersey Turnpike.

"I got a call from a friend of mine who was down there. Some of the guys from the Jersey unions were trying to get across on a tugboat, which was ferrying people away from the disaster to Jersey. I made my way down there by back roads and jumped on a tugboat that was returning for more passengers."

All over the city, construction workers like Eamonn Carey were responding to the crisis. Almost every ironworker downed tools on whatever job he was working on and rushed to the site. Elsewhere, construction men raced across the Brooklyn Bridge in a mad dash to try to help, against the tide of humanity who were trying to flood out of the city.

Like the firefighters and police, they rushed in when others were fleeing away in deadly fear of their lives. They were fearless, yet deadly afraid, as Eamonn Carey says, uncertain of what would happen once they went to work on the eight-storey-high pile. They were the unsung heroes of the rescue efforts, unpaid, unconcerned for their own safety and totally committed to finding survivors of the dreadful tragedy.

When he arrived, Carey remembers an atmosphere of pure chaos. "When we got there, we had no protection, no masks, anything. We started pulling away the lighter pieces of rubble by hand. Everyone started from the same spot, a narrow opening on the north end of the rubble. "It was the only place we had access to. Nowhere else was stable."

They commenced the frantic scramble to find any survivors. "We needed to pull away as much rubble as possible to allow the ironworkers to get in to burn steel. We were throwing body parts out of the way in our haste. It was a truly hideous scene," he says.

Rumours ran rampant: there were 500 commuters trapped alive in the subway station underneath the inferno; up to 30,000 people were likely caught in the rubble. Everywhere there was confusion.

"A lot of the surface fires had been dealt with," he recalls, "but awful fires were raging beneath, making rescue work even harder." A dense smoke hung in the air, causing choking and coughing. Visibility was just a few yards, and the rescue effort was still just being organised.

The bodies and body parts were everywhere. "A lot of people we found were people who were running away from the towers when they collapsed. Some were killed by flying glass. There was no mark on them, but when you lifted them the body collapsed like jelly."

A human chain, using buckets, began to remove the debris, stopping every time they thought they heard a cry or a banging from the rubble. Dogs were immediately brought in, but the number of survivors found were few and far between. All night Carey worked at the coal face, barely stopping to take a breather, but the inevitable impact of what had occurred was beginning to sink in.

The firefighters there, while present physically, were so shell-shocked at losing so many colleagues that they could barely talk. Many were weeping openly. A pall of gloom hung over the site, punctuated by occasional cries for sniffer dogs and, more often, the loud explosion of cars trapped in the rubble blowing up as the underground fires reached them.

"I worked till I dropped," Carey says. "It was exhausting, backbreaking work, and we knew the chances of finding people were getting slimmer by the hour." He remembers, finally, being forced to take a break and making it home to New Jersey at 4 o'clock on Wednesday morning, 12 September. "I went home, took my clothes off, threw them away, took a shower, picked up a few others guys and went straight back in."

He went back to a disaster site that had become even more dangerous in his brief absence. Massive shifts in the rubble meant that no one was safe. In addition, the fires and the unseasonably hot weather meant that the stench on the site had worsened considerably since he had left. Still the search for survivors continued.

Finally, at 10.30 that morning, two people were pulled out alive, one on the north side of the wreckage, one on the south side. "A worker heard a banging and the dogs were brought in. A human chain carried the woman to the waiting ambulance. I don't know if she made it," says Carey about the victim he helped bring out. "She looked in very bad shape."

Later that day a fire captain called for volunteers to work with firefighters on the highly dangerous task of climbing into the rubble and seeking survivors there. Carey volunteered and immediately found himself climbing into pockets in the rubble in search of anyone still breathing.

He shudders at the memory of what he had to do. "You had to get into every nook and cranny. Any time you found a hole in the rubble, you dropped in with your torch. The likelihood of injury was great because the pile was constantly shifting and the cars caught in the rubble were still exploding.

"The holes were 20 to 30 feet deep sometimes, and you were lowered down on a rope with a torch. It was not like going down a manhole or a pothole; it was full of jagged edges, debris, steel bars rubbing against you. I was very scared working down there. It is pitch black, the stench is terrible, and as you were hauling away loose debris to see what was underneath, you knew the pile could shift underneath you and kill you instantly. It was like a horror movie; you wait for the big moment, your heart is racing, wondering what you will find. You're almost afraid to find anybody. The claustrophobia, the feeling of being hemmed in, was awful. Yet you had to keep doing it again and again."

He estimated he climbed into 20 to 30 holes on that Wednesday and Thursday. By then the hopes of finding survivors was fading fast. The dogs were no longer needed, because the smell of decomposing bodies was everywhere. The only thing that kept the rescuers going was the hope that somehow, in one of the cavities, someone had survived.

"I ended up with a guy from Rescue 4 fire company who had lost several colleagues. We were going through the roof of a garage that had collapsed, but we couldn't find any bodies." They found six bodies in a collapsed gym, where he believes the people had fled to or were working out. It was grim work.

On Friday, FEMA, the Federal Emergency Management Agency, took over the searching, and what had been an all-volunteer effort suddenly became a much more organised and security-conscious operation.

Carey understood the need for tighter security. "Until FEMA, all you needed to get on the site was a pair of balls and a union card," he says. "There were people down there, not to help, but looking for wallets and rings, real ghouls." He himself had an encounter with an English tabloid journalist who had stolen a hard hat and somehow bluffed his way on to the site.

"We were bringing out the body of a fireman from under the north tower. Suddenly a flash went off behind us. We saw this guy, with a hard hat and a knapsack in which he was collecting debris. He was from one of the English tabloid newspapers. One of the firemen, he was about 6 ft 5 tall, tackled him and beat the shit out of him, smashed his camera and handed him over to the cops. He was lucky he wasn't killed."

When FEMA came on the scene, everything changed. Workers now were hired by construction companies contracted to get the work done. "Unless you were hired by one of the firms you could not get on to the site," says Carey. "You couldn't just volunteer any more. It changed a lot of things for everyone."

On Friday morning, Carey and his friends were turned back when they turned up to volunteer. "We went home and got drunk, got drunk for a week. We didn't get drunk because of what we saw down there; it was actually about being turned away on the Friday. It was like someone had pulled the rug from under us. We were definitely willing to continue as volunteers, but we were replaced with guys who were just looking for a paycheck. It was too early to do that, things were still not organised. They should have let it go to Monday instead of saying, 'We don't need you.' "

How is he coping with the death and destruction that he witnessed? "You have to cope with everything. For the first couple of months, it was not something I was able to forget; but at the same time I can't wish it never happened. I'd still be the first one to jump in a car if something similar happened again."

He says one of his proudest moments was bringing the Irish flag from his home in New Jersey and planting it at Ground Zero along with the Stars and Stripes. "I just felt there were so many Irish involved, both among the dead and the rescuers, that it felt right. We were very proud of that flag."

He remembers, too, the intense camaraderie that working on the site brought about. "I'd regard myself as very lucky; two of my best friends were with me. We grew very close. No one else could understand you after, what you had seen and all, but I know I can call them up and talk about it.

"I wasn't going to go home for Christmas because of what happened. I could not see myself sitting in John B. Keane's pub in Listowel and telling people at home what it was really like. It was not time for that. But it wasn't too bad when I got back."

So does he consider himself a hero? "No, not at all. The firemen were the heroes. They knew it was a good day to die.

They told me the priest who gave Mychal Judge, the fire brigade chaplain, the last rites turned around after it and was faced with a group of firefighters looking for absolution before going into the fire. Not one of them ever came out. Every one of them was a hero; they were men who knew what was in store. I can't put myself in the same category as those guys."

There is another moment he remembers fondly, after two days of non-stop work. "We were leaving the site, and we were so tired we could hardly walk. We were lugging all our tools. These emergency workers gave us a lift in their ambulance to 14th Street, where the Welcome Highway began. When we got out of the ambulance, we were stormed, hugged and kissed, given food and water by the people who were there to cheer on the rescue workers. I broke down and cried like a baby."

THE IRONWORKER

Jack Doyle was only 26 in 1970 when a small crew of ironworkers braved the bitter cold and howling winds and raised an American flag at the top of the World Trade Center's north tower.

The moment stayed with him ever after, he told the *Irish Voice* newspaper. "It was like you were making history. You could see the Statue of Liberty, the Empire State Building, and I was higher than that. You do this when you are only 26, and you think, 'I'm on top of the world.' And you are."

Doyle spent some 18 months working on the project, from the ground floor all the way up to the 110th storey. The ironworkers handled over 200,000 tons of steel in building the landmark.

Doyle was one of many Newfoundland Irish who took part. He was born in Newfoundland and moved to Brooklyn and became an ironworker in 1962. For Newfoundlanders, joining the Ironworkers' Local is as common as Irish

carpenters joining Local 608, the big union that has
employed thousands of them over the years.

The Ironworkers' Union is heavily composed of those
from Newfoundland and of Mohawk Indians. "No one else
is crazy enough to do what they do," says an Irish construction worker who has often worked with them.

The jobs they do are incredibly dangerous, as they hover
out over thin air to put a steel beam in place. The early films
of New York celebrate the ironworkers building the skyscrapers, their extraordinary courage as they balanced on
thin beams only inches wide a thousand feet off the ground.
It was no job for the fainthearted, then or now.

Jack Doyle has risen through the ranks since his moment
helping to plant the flag atop the World Trade Center tower
and is now the president and business agent of Local 40,
which represents 1,500 ironworkers.

Like him, many former workers from that time were
back at the World Trade Center right after 11 September.
What was left of the towers they so proudly built, they now
had to tear down. Right after the collapse, the first call that
went out was for the ironworkers, who were desperately
needed to try to prise or torch apart the massive steel beams
that had become a mausoleum for all trapped beneath.

With fires burning and chaos reigning, the ironworkers
worked steadily and methodically. With gobs of Vick in their
noses to mask the stench of death, they searched and drove
through the rubble, all day and night long, day after day.

Whenever bodies were found, they were there with their
torches, waiting to melt down or slice through steel that was
proving an impediment.

"It was very slow moving," says Doyle. "We couldn't
just go in and do what we were good at." He is proud, however, that his men have played such a role. Many in fact had
just walked off other jobsites on 11 September and gone to
volunteer. "There was still an enormous amount of heat
there. There was steel you could not touch, but still they
came."

Doyle says that, despite their experience and their high-
risk profession, some of the men he sent down could not

handle the sights and sounds of Ground Zero. "We've had guys who just had to give up. It was pretty gruesome."

It could have been much worse for some of them, of course. "Just a month before, we had 12 or 15 working up on the antenna on the north tower," says Doyle. "They were lucky the job was finished."

During the grim times as the ironworkers toiled day after day trying to clear the site, Doyle says that one thought kept many of them going long after the hope of finding anyone alive was gone. The ultimate project for the men was to help rebuild the site. They lived for that opportunity.

"We'll see what they replace it with," says Doyle. "It would be great to see the twin towers back, just to be defiant. The workers talk about helping rebuild it all the time."

If they do, Jack Doyle will be one person who will have plenty of experience of such a building perched high above the Manhattan canyons. Doyle says the original trade centre project was not that dangerous, despite the stunning heights.

"Believe it or not, it was a safer job than an average skyscraper. Much of the assembling was done on the street and then hoisted up into place." Other work was done inside the building shell so there was not much need for ironworkers to hang from perilous heights. Meanwhile, huge ocean barges and even helicopters ferried in huge chunks of the building. Of course, there were serious injuries, too. Doyle's own brother, George, fell and was seriously injured.

Even the hardened ironworker found it hard to come to terms with what happened on 11 September. But the band of brothers, including Doyle, want to stay involved even in such a grim task. "If we can build a new World Trade Center and hang the star spangled banner at the top, it will all be worth it for us," he says with a smile.

CHAPTER TWENTY-FOUR

"WE HAVE A GRAVE TO GO TO THERE"

MIKE MEEHAN HAD a unique way to lull his children to sleep. The Donegal immigrant had seven sons and two daughters, all living in a fourth-floor walk-up in the Inwood section of Manhattan, not a stone's throw from Gaelic Park, home of Gaelic football in the United States.

As they tossed and turned trying to sleep at night, Mike would recite an imaginary commentary on a big GAA match being played, which prominently featured the Meehan boys. "I'd usually do it on the weekends when they had no school," Mike remembers. "I'd do the commentary as I put them to bed."

"Shaun Meehan has the ball, he passes to Michael Meehan; Michael Meehan moves it downfield, he passes it to Eugene; he takes it and sends it across the field to Kevin. It's downfield now to Chris Meehan. He passes it to Paul Meehan, and he sends it to Damian Meehan. He kicks – it's over the bar."

Damian, the youngest boy, always took care of the winning score when he was put to bed, a fond tribute from a father who dreamt of having his children follow in his footsteps with his love of Irish football.

Of all of them, Damian came closest to his dreams. A highly talented athlete, he became a star on the Good Shepherd team, culled from the parish the Meehans lived in. Good Shepherd was started in the 1940s. It was a time when there were no fewer than 12 Gaelic football teams on the island of Manhattan. Undoubtedly their finest day was in 1947 when the All-Ireland final was played for the first and only time outside Ireland. Good Shepherd, from the parish of Inwood, composed of all Irish American kids, played in the opening match that day, a proud moment for the yellow and blue.

From eight years old on, Damian worked his way up through the underage Good Shepherd sides, making Gaelic football his first love, despite the massive popularity of baseball and football in his neighbourhood.

He was talented, too; good enough to play for the New York team for three years at a time when the immigrant plane had brought many highly skilled native Irish footballers to American shores and to Gaelic Park in New York. When Good Shepherd folded in 1996, because there were not enough players to field a team, Damian switched to his father's ancestral team, Donegal, a perennial powerhouse in Gaelic Park.

As a "narrowback", Damian started with an inherent disadvantage, not having the same exposure to the game growing up as Irish-born players had, but he was a quick learner.

Former teammate John McDonald remembers "a classy performer" who would easily have played county football at the highest levels in Ireland. In the 1993 New York final, he was man of the match.

Terry Connaughton, a Roscommon native, whose son Terry Junior was also a star on the Good Shepherd team, remembers Damian as one of the finest footballers he has ever seen in New York. "I doubt if we would have had the same success without him. He seemed to inspire all those around him," he says. In the Division 2 final in 1995, the *Irish Voice* reporter wrote that "Good Shepherd could not have asked for more from Damian Meehan."

For Mike Meehan, to whom Gaelic games occupied a level only a notch below heaven, Damian's expertise at the game was God-given. He brags about the medals his son won. "I can't tell you how many, because there were so many on the walls. Damian was a great player and loved the Gaelic

Park scene." The plaques of his achievements and those of his brothers now line the walls of the Meehans' four-bedroomed apartment.

Perhaps his toughness as an athlete was nurtured growing up as the second youngest in a family of nine and receiving all the inevitable knocks a child at the tail end of a family endures. Yet Mike remembers he was hardly a problem. "He was as solid as a rock. He was loving and placid. You know, he grew up to love his older brothers more than they loved themselves."

The story of Mike Meehan from Donegal town and his wife Peg from nearby Drimarone begins in 1950s Ireland when the emigrant boat was the only ticket out. In Coventry, England, in 1954, 18-year-old Mike, then a worker at the Jaguar Motor Company, first laid eyes on Peg, a nurse, at an Irish dance at the Westfield House. It was, according to both partners, love at first sight; but as usual, the path did not run entirely smoothly.

They returned to Donegal to nurse Peg's mother, Jane Meehan. On the morning they were to depart for America, on 10 October 1957, her mother died. Mike had to go ahead and board the ship in Cork, and Peg came six months later.

This time New York was the destination, a buzzing new Irish enclave called Inwood in upper Manhattan. Inwood was a typical New York neighbourhood where friends, relatives and neighbours all lived cheek by jowl, most in huge apartment blocks unlike the farms they had left behind in Ireland. The closeness was both a refuge and a boon for new immigrants seeking their first foothold.

Not that Inwood was merely a sea of concrete and urban blight. Near their home was Inwood Hill Park, 196 acres almost untouched since the first pilgrims arrived. It is the only untouched patch of Manhattan Island left. It was where the Dutch bought the island from the Indians for a few trinkets, and it was a wonderland for the Meehan kids.

The park also had a football field for the sons of immigrants. Peg Meehan never missed a game any of her sons played.

Peg and Mike were married on 27 February 1960, at

Notre Dame in nearby Morningside Heights. Following the wedding there was a reception at the legendary Trocadero ballroom on Dyckman Street at Vermilya Avenue, where many Irish matches were made and weddings celebrated. The celebrations and the old songs lasted well into the evening. They spent their honeymoon night in a Manhattan hotel. Nine months later, almost to the day, their first child was born.

At the time there was an explosion of emigration from Ireland, hundreds of thousands fleeing harsh economic times. Not since the aftermath of the Irish Civil War 30 years earlier had there been anything like it.

Now the cold winds blew again. Most of the emigration was from the large western seaboard counties: Mayo, Donegal, Kerry, Galway, Cork, mainly the sons and daughters of small farmers who faced a desperate future with no prospects other than emigration.

The women emigrated alongside the men, something unique to the Irish in Europe, where most other countries emigrated on a ratio of three men to every woman.

It meant that the enclaves they built persisted longer, that the bonds of blood and soil extended far beyond the immediate generation. Families were as close in Inwood as they were in any village in Ireland. The centre of all activity was the parish church of Good Shepherd, a warm hearth in an often-cold world. Mike and Peg Meehan threw themselves wholeheartedly into the community.

Mike Meehan remembers that when he'd go to mass on Sundays, he'd meet as many from home as if he were back in Donegal; and his wife remembers that despite their own large brood, there was always a pullout couch for visitors from the old sod. "The bed never got cold," she says.

For the kids, the seven boys and two girls who arrived within ten years, Inwood was their corner of Ireland and America, as remote from downtown Manhattan as Donegal from Dublin.

There was also another slice of Ireland in their lives. Catering to their ever-growing family, Mike and Peg Meehan purchased some land in Accord, New York, in 1974, in the midst of the Irish Catskills resort area. There they built their dream summer home, far from the bustle of the big city some three hours to the south. The green and rolling hills and clear mountain air reminded Mike and Peg of home, and Mike christened his new house "The Four Green Fields". The kids loved it as a summer escape from the city and played Gaelic football with their friends and went swimming and hiking.

Damian graduated from St Raymond's High School in 1987. After attending the State University at New Paltz after graduation, he continued his education at Lehman College, not far from his home. At Lehman his youngest sister Janine introduced him to Joann McCarthy, a pretty blond from Moshulu Park, who shared a similar close-knit Irish background. Her parents had emigrated from Dingle, County Kerry.

"Joann was so taken with Damian and he with her," remembers Mike Meehan. "Oh, they had a couple of breakups, but they always found their way back to each other."

Damian and Joann married in June of 1998 at Mount St Ursula's in the Bronx in front of 100 family members and friends. If Damian had had his way the couple might have eloped. "He was such a quiet soul, he was not into the fanfare," Mike says. "He was going to try to elope and get married in Las Vegas, but Joann insisted on a proper wedding."

By then, unlike most of his brothers who went into construction, the police department and the fire department, Damian had taken a different track.

In the early 1980s a tradition had begun in Inwood unlike any before. Young men and women from the area began working on Wall Street, an unheard-of occurrence for Bronx Irish kids. Marty Boyle, Damian's brother-in-law, was among the first to hear that there was a very good living to be made. None of the Inwood boys had any college education worth speaking of, but the real education was on the street, which fitted working on Wall Street, Marty remembers, because, "You're constantly yelling and screaming with people every day."

Marty Boyle says up to 40 Inwood people worked in and

around the Commodities Exchange, making more money than their immigrant parents ever dreamed of. Marty wasn't long convincing his brother-in-law Damian that a move downtown was worth it.

Ironically it was in 1993, just after the twin towers were attacked for the first time, that Damian began his new career at Carr Futures, a financial trading institution based in the World Trade Center.

Damian found the hurly-burly on the floor too much to bear, however. "He wasn't very noisy or boisterous," according to his father. He moved into a backroom job at Carr where he proved very successful. Brendan Dolan, an Inwood friend with whom he played Gaelic football, made sure he was looked after.

Meanwhile he had settled into his domestic life after his marriage to Joann. They first lived in Riverdale, not far from their parents. They scrimped and saved and moved to Glen Rock, New Jersey, an affluent suburb close to several fellow workers, most notably his former Gaelic football colleagues Joe Holland and Brendan Dolan. "I bought the cheapest house on the most expensive block," Damian told his father, and the rest of the clan rallied round to put the house in shape for the happy couple.

Damian Peter Meehan Junior was born on 23 January 2000, the 17th grandchild for Mike and Peg Meehan. Damian's wife remembers that after bringing the baby home from the hospital how much more confident Damian was in handling him than she was.

Indeed, he was so preoccupied with his son that he gave up his beloved Gaelic football because he could no longer commit to the two nights of training a week that was the requirement. "Damian was an unbelievable father," Mike Meehan recalls fondly. "I think it was because he had grown up in such a large family."

On the weekend before 11 September, Damian and Joann Meehan enjoyed a rare treat, a getaway for themselves to Spring Lake, often called the Irish Riviera, on the Jersey shore. Mike and Peg looked after young Damian at the Glen Rock home.

It was a glorious early autumn weekend, and the couple enjoyed their time before returning to Glen Rock on the afternoon of 10 September. Mike and Peg declined a dinner invitation and decided to return home to Inwood.

The next morning started out like any other. Mike, an early riser, turned on his regular news programme and discovered to his horror that a plane had hit the World Trade Center. He immediately called Joann to see if Damian had left for work – he was sometimes late leaving the house. Joann told him that he had and had barely made his train after rising late.

Mike and his family watched in horror as the second plane hit the other tower, and they began fearing the worst. Then they received what they believed was a hopeful call from Eugene, Damian's brother, who was a firefighter in the Bronx.

Damian was working on the 92nd floor, just one below where the plane had hit. He called Eugene and told him he was fine, but that there was a lot of smoke in the building and he was seeking advice on how to get out. Eugene told him to see where the smoke was coming from and to take the opposite direction to it. It was the last time anyone would ever hear from Damian.

"We don't know what happened then," says Mike, his voice breaking. "Damian was a superb athlete – he ran in 5k and 10k races – so we have great difficulty understanding why someone as fit as him wasn't able to make it out. We've rehashed it many times. There were 71 people in Carr and none of them got out. There had to be a serious obstacle in the way."

Damian, in fact, came closest. His body was found on a much lower floor, surrounded by firemen. Mike believes that somehow he had found a way around whatever obstruction was blocking the stairwells and had almost made it out. It made the loss that much harder to bear.

"11 September was an awful day of watching TV, hoping we'd see Damian running down the street," says Mike. "By late afternoon, when we hadn't heard from him, we had a sinking feeling we would not be getting any good news".

A long and terrible night followed. The next day, sensing the worst, the family fanned out to every hospital where there were reports of victims being brought, in the desperate hope that they could discover Damian alive. They had no luck.

"After Damian was gone, we wondered how and if he suffered," says Mike. "There was no smoke inhalation, his death certificate says he died from blunt trauma. It's still too hard to understand."

For the first few weeks, before the body was found, Joann found it impossible to believe her husband was dead. "Joann was in denial the first two weeks. She was expecting him to walk through the door," says Mike.

Then came the call at 4 a.m. one early October morning. The body had been found intact. The parents, who had gone to mass every day hoping and praying the body of their son would turn up, felt that a huge burden had been lifted from them.

The wake and mass at Good Shepherd, the centre of so much of his formative years, was held on 8 October 2001. At least 4,000 people showed up, as that number of mortuary cards were taken. The lines ran so long around the funeral home that local restaurants brought food to those waiting because they were going to be outside for hours.

They buried Damian in his father's plot in upstate New York, near their vacation home. It was where Mike and his family had found the most peace, and it seemed fitting that Damian would rest for ever there now. Several members of the family live permanently in the area.

"We've had the best of times up here," says Mike Meehan, "enjoying all the kids, growing up together, just resting and relaxing. It will always be a special place for us. You know. We're just going day by day, now, dealing with things in the best way we know how."

Just how much Damian was loved became clear again a few weeks later. On Sunday, 25 November, just two days after Thanksgiving, which had to be the toughest ever holiday for the Meehan family, his friends got together to honour Damian one last time and to create an educational fund for his children and those of his colleague and friend, Joe

Kellet. Damian and Joe had played together on the Good Shepherd Gaelic football team which won so many titles at nearby Gaelic Park. In death, as in life, the two fast friends were united in a common bond.

That evening the crowds spilled out on to the streets outside the Riverdale Steak House in Riverdale, the leafy neighbourhood which borders the Hudson River on one side and the less pleasant side of the Bronx on the other. Despite a pelting rain that threatened a flash flood, the patrons kept coming and coming to pay tribute to Damian and Joe, the two young Inwood natives who lost their lives at the World Trade Center.

From 4 o'clock until 8 the friends of Damian and Joe gathered in the bar, in the restaurant, down in the cellar, out the backyard, and even out the front in the pouring rain.

The weather hardly seemed to matter. As Terry Connaughton, owner of the Riverdale Steak House and a close friend of the Meehan family, said, "This is a tribute to the families and how much these young men were loved."

The expectation had been that up to $20,000 would be raised for an educational fund for the children. In fact, the final total was over $70,000.

"It is very, very difficult to lose a son," says Mike Meehan now. "Over the years I've lost my parents and other family members, but I feel in one way it is easier for me and Peg to deal with it, than for his brothers and sisters. It has been very, very difficult.

"I think of him often in his Good Shepherd jersey, coming down the field with the ball. I wish I could see him again, just once, to tell him how much we love him and miss him. He always had a kind word for everybody, and until he died we never fully realised just how much he was loved."

On 13 January, Madison Margaret Meehan came into the world, a healthy and beautiful little girl. "She looks just like Damian," says her proud grandfather Mike Meehan. "She is truly a gift from God."

CHAPTER TWENTY-FIVE

A TRIBUTE TO MATTIE O

FOR TWO DAYS at the start of October 2001, the healing power of music worked its magic on a grieving city badly in need of emotional sustenance. From Ground Zero to a memorial service on Park Avenue, Paddy Moloney and the Chieftains inspired those who heard them with a tribute to all who died, and especially to a young man who called himself their "number one fan".

Of all the performances the Chieftains have played, the band would surely agree that the most moving one they've ever given came on the bright Wednesday morning of 3 October, in a Catholic church on Park Avenue in Manhattan. It wasn't a happy occasion, but the Chieftains did their part to make the memorial service for Matthew O'Mahony, a 39-year-old merchant banker for Cantor Fitzgerald who was killed on 11 September, as much of a joyous celebration of his short life as it could possibly be.

As it turns out, Matthew O'Mahony regarded himself as the Chieftains' number one American fan. He never missed any of the band's concerts in New York, and their music was a staple in the house he shared with his wife Lauren Murphy, a publicist for the Island Record label, which has a number of top artists on its roster.

It was Lauren's music industry contacts that had brought her into contact with her late husband's favourite band. She had met them before when they appeared on the popular late night TV show fronted by David Letterman. But Lauren could never have reckoned that she would someday make a call to Paddy Moloney, requesting the band to play some of Matthew's favourite songs at his memorial. The Chieftains immediately said yes.

"About two weeks ago Lauren called our office," Paddy said at the service, which was filled with thousands of mourners. "She told us about Matty O and how he had loved our band. She said she would love nothing better than for us to play at his memorial service. We said we would come. I didn't really know him, but I have gotten to know him in the last few days. I tell you, I would have loved to have gone for a pint with him."

The Chieftains played a number of songs and airs at the service which helped to ease Lauren's grief. "Have I Told You Lately That I Love You?" brought a smile to the young widow's face, and at communion the band brought their own unique musical talents to "Danny Boy".

"Lauren asked us to play it," Paddy says. "It wasn't one of ours, but it sounded great in the church. It was a personal touch. She said he loved the song."

Her husband's love of Ireland seemed to be always on his mind, no matter what he was doing or where he was. He loved working in Cantor Fitzgerald's New York headquarters high atop one of the world's most famous buildings and swore to his friends that on a clear day he could see the mountains of Ireland from his 95th floor office. Lauren and Matthew were married for two years. When Matthew decided to pop the question, he had brought her to Ireland.

Before the service began, Moloney held Lauren's hand as she spoke with all the mourners, offering words of comfort. At the end, the church choir sang Van Morrison's "God Shine His Light on Me", another one of Matthew's Irish favourites. The Chieftains brought the service to a close with "Limerick's Lamentation". Matthew O'Mahony would have been honoured.

"It's so hard to say goodbye," Matthew's best friend Adam Levy said. "I can't imagine what life will be like without him. The only words that can describe him were Yeats':

'Think where man's glory most begins and ends. And say my glory was, I had such friends.'"

Paddy Moloney was so emotionally moved by his first visit to New York since the 11 September attacks that he felt the need to bring his tin whistle to Ground Zero to pay a personal homage to those who perished. "When I left the service I knew my work here was not done," Moloney told the *Irish Voice* newspaper. Moloney and his daughter Aedín visited the World Trade Center site the following day. He gained access to the immediate Ground Zero area through a police officer whose grandparents were from Cork and who was familiar with his music.

Workers all around were still coming to grips with the unimaginable devastation and desperately searching for the thousands of victims lying among the ruins. Heavy-lifting machinery made thundering noises, but the soothing airs Moloney played rose above the devastation and provided a few needed minutes of comfort for those who stopped work to listen.

"I hadn't planned to play those tunes; I hadn't rehearsed. That often happens – you get inspired at that very split second.

"Then as I played I felt I saw them, all the faces, faces without images. The mechanics of the music disappeared and my heart went into it. I got the shivers up my back."

He played the Irish wake song "Táimse 'mo Chodladh" (I am asleep, don't wake me), and the lament "Dóchas" (hope).

"Music is not just mechanical. It is like a living thing. It starts to come into you, and that happened to me here," Moloney told *The Irish Times* after his performance.

He departed back home on a flight that evening, feeling that he contributed to New York's recovery effort in the best way he knew how. For Matthew O'Mahony's relatives and his wife Lauren, the Chieftains' presence made the painful day a little bit easier to bear. For the Chieftains it was an opportunity to contribute in their own small way to a healing process for a city and a family devastated by the events of 11 September.

CHAPTER TWENTY-SIX

LIZ SMITH'S LOSS

L IZ SMITH, 34, is seated in Jameson's restaurant in downtown Rockaway, just a stone's throw from the beach and also from the location where the American Airlines jet crashed a few weeks after 11 September.

The pub is a typical Irish watering hole with friendly bar staff and, on this Saturday morning, almost deserted. At the bar two or three regulars sip their drinks while occasionally watching a basketball game on the several television sets.

Liz Smith has brought along a childhood friend, Martin McManus, to help her remember the good times when she and her boyfriend Mike Andrews, who died at the World Trade Center, double-dated with Marty and his wife.

The two have remained close friends; and she relies on Marty, who knew Mike since they were toddlers, to fill in any of the early details. Marty smiles frequently as he recalls the childhood memories, but tears are not far away either when he discusses his best friend's fate on 11 September.

If you were to pick an All American looking girl, Liz Smith would be it: blonde hair, blue eyes and a cheerleader's figure. In fact, she is a former model, and nowadays, in addition to her guidance counsellor job at a school in Queens, she has a successful side business in photography and art.

After Mike died, she sent a card to many of the friends who had helped her, which she designed and photographed herself. It is the words "Thank You" scrawled on the sand at Rockaway Beach as the tide rushes in.

Liz Smith's world fell apart on 11 September when her boyfriend and soon-to-be husband Mike Andrews, a broker with the firm of Cantor Fitzgerald, never came out of the World Trade Center towers.

A year earlier Liz Smith had lost her brother, who was killed in the course of a mugging, so she certainly knows what tragedy feels like. Yet she remains resilient, much more focused on the good memories than the bad, in public anyway, though she sometimes breaks down. She tells of her last night and morning with Mike, her Rockaway sweetheart.

"Mike left Tuesday morning; he had stayed over at my house. The night before I cooked dinner for him, which was a bit of a joke between us, as I hadn't cooked for him much. He e-mailed me on Monday to ask if I had been struck by lightning.

"I cooked him a nice family dinner, shrimp and pasta, tomatoes. My whole family insisted on coming over when they heard I was cooking. I remember standing in the kitchen talking to them, and I said, 'You must think I'm Jesus, but I don't know how to feed you all with a loaf and some fish.'

"Mike went to bed early to watch the New York Jets football game, and I remember we battled over the remote and what we would watch after. It was just a lovely easy night.

"The next day, 11 September, as he left the house he said, 'I love you,' and kissed me, and I gave him a kiss goodbye. On my way to work I realised he had put gas in my car the night before and I wanted to call him to thank him, but I said I'd leave it until he got to work.

"I work as a guidance counsellor. I cross the Broad Channel Bridge every day, and I see the twin towers. I remember it was such a gorgeous day and the city looked beautiful.

"When I got to work, which is in a very small office, I was talking about what I had cooked for dinner the night before to Barbara, the other counsellor. Suddenly the phone rang, and Barbara picked it up and said, 'What?' And next thing I knew she threw down the phone, and I said, 'What happened?' and she said a plane had crashed into the twin towers, and I remember her getting up and running across to the teachers' room.

"She came running back in and I couldn't move, and I kept looking at her and screaming, 'Which tower? Which tower?' And she said the one with the things on top. I knew then it was bad, because I had once asked Mike, 'How do I know which tower you work in so I know where to find you?' and he said, 'The one with the antenna on top.'

"I walked into the teachers' room and looked at the television and I turned round. I ran back and dialled Mike's number, and it kept ringing and ringing and ringing – a good sign, I thought, as he was probably on his way out. 'He knows what's going on,' I thought. So I just kept dialling and dialling. Nobody at work had realised that Mike worked on the 105th floor. I just knew it was bad, very bad. I called his dad, who tried to calm me down. 'Mike will get out. We may not hear for a while,' he told me.

"Then everybody began calling; they were hysterical which made me worse. They were finding it very hard to get through to me. It was just unbelievable."

Here she stops to collect herself, the memory of the tragedy and that awful day flooding back. When she resumes she wants to tell me all about the man she loved and not to focus on the events of 11 September.

"I knew him a long time from Rockaway. We were born just six days apart. We had the same friends, same Irish background. He was born on 10 January 1967. I guess we always flirted, always attracted to each other. He asked me out one time, and I told him I had to babysit. He never let me live it down.

"Then three years ago he said, 'Why can't we just go out?' and I said, for some stupid reason, 'Send me a card,' and Marty here had to come down my block to get the address. And the card read, "Even though you are a pain in the ass, I'd like to go out with you.' So I called him and said I'd like to, too.

"When we were on our tenth date, my brother was killed. He was mugged, and Mike was amazing to me. My brother's death was devastating to me, never having lost anyone else before. The way it happened, after that I thought I was safe, my bad luck was over.

"We had two and a half years together, and we did a lot of things. I have pictures and memories that will always give me happiness, knowing that he was happy.

"He was a very hard worker, very determined to get ahead, that was his focus, and it annoyed me sometimes. I wanted to do other things, so we had broken up for a few months because I thought he was such a workaholic. That turned out okay, though, because he realised what was important. He knew that he wanted to spend the rest of his life with me. He sent Marty down to my house to tell me. He was the nicest guy you would wanna meet.

"We were about to get engaged that week. We had talked about getting married in May. A friend of his on the 103rd floor at work let me know after he died that he had made all the plans. Looking back, he wanted everything perfect. A perfect ring and the perfect time – that was Mike.

"I am so glad that on 8 September I threw a party for him. I'm a big party person. It was 'Bring your funniest photo,' and I had one of Mike with a ridiculous wig on. I had had this picture for so long, and something made me have this party, and I blew up the picture to unveil it.

"That was the best day. We did everything together. We went shopping; we went to Long Beach for a volleyball game. It was a great day. I came home and had to take a nap because the sun had given me a headache and I wasn't feeling well. I woke up three hours later in a panic, but he had done everything, decorated the yard, picked up the food, all that. A lot of people had a conversation with him that day. One of my girlfriends said to him about us, 'What are you waiting for?' and he joked, 'If she didn't have that damned dog we'd be engaged right now.'

"Mike was one of seven siblings, four boys and three girls, in the Andrews' house. They are a great Irish family, very strong. What is important is good schooling, good basics, the epitome of a good stand-up family.

"It's very tough for them without Mike, but the siblings are strong. Everyone grieves differently. Mike was very close to his parents. He and his father were big Yankee and Notre Dame fans. Even if there were beach parties planned, he'd often cancel and just sit home with his dad watching the game.

"He had a big heart. I remember once in a restaurant an older woman who didn't look well off at all was eating dinner alone when we were eating, and when we finished Mike paid her bill, too. That's what he was like.

"Our families got on very well. My mom feels she has lost another son. His friends from work have been wonderful. They have helped keep me going. I don't think people fully realise the calibre of people who were lost, real leaders in this community.

"This has brought people in Rockaway closer together. The people of Rockaway have shown me and others tremendous support. It has gotten us all through. Without it we could not have taken a step forward. It's one of the good things to come out of all this.

"I have to say I take a couple of steps forward, then things that happen take steps from under you. Not having found the body, it's almost a part of this that makes it all surreal and as if Mike is away on some vacation.

"I have a side business. I'm very driven, but I dread the New Year because I don't know how I will keep going. I think of him all the time: when I'm lifting the 15 pound bag of dog food (he'd usually grab it off me), when I'm in the car and I think, 'I have to call Mike.'

"But I have learnt most of all not to take anything for granted. Always tell the people closest to you you love them. I'm so thankful for the dinner the night before, for that kiss that morning. It all makes you realise you have to stop and smell the roses. He was learning that.

"It's not going to knock me down. I know nobody can fix my heart. I've lost the man I was going to spend the rest of my life with. It's unfair. I died on 11 September, and yet I'm still here walking. I have a lot of love and family and friends, but it's tough.

"People tell you how with time you can handle this better. I don't know. He understood me like no one else. I could talk to him every day. I still do, in fact. My business has been doing very well, and I know he's responsible.

"In a way I'm glad I never got to speak to him when the planes hit. I wouldn't have wanted to if I heard any fear in his voice. That's not how I remember him. He told me there were only two things in life he was afraid of: snakes and kryptonite. And that's how I want to remember him."

CHAPTER TWENTY-SEVEN

NEWFOUNDLAND, 11 SEPTEMBER

ENIS KELLEHER, 62, had stopped off in Gander, Newfoundland, in 1958 on his way to America. It was the era before there were direct flights, and Gander was the first landfall. For the raw 18-year-old, it was the first step on his great North American adventure.

Since that time, the County Kerry native from near Killarney had flown over Newfoundland on hundreds of occasions, but it had never occurred to him that he would ever land on the rocky outcrop on the Canadian coast again.

He had come a long way from the shy son of a shoemaker who had first set foot on North American soil all those years ago and had achieved spectacular success in America. He began as a messenger boy on Wall Street, but helped by sympathetic traders and his own hard work, he had broken into the world of high finance. He had risen to the top in several Wall Street firms and eventually branched out on his own. His current company, Wall Street Access, a discount brokerage of which he was founder and chief shareholder, had been valued at over $1 billion dollars in one newspaper report.

His friends now numbered many among the richest and most powerful in America. He was chairman of St John's University in New York, one of the great centres of learning in the city, and he was a highly sought after fundraiser for charitable causes.

He also retained an active interest in Irish causes. He had

been one of the first backers of the Irish Immigration Reform Movement, committed to helping Irish illegals become green card holders and American citizens. He had also hosted many of Northern Ireland's top political leaders, from both sides of the spectrum, at private lunches in his spectacular Wall Street offices which overlooked the Statue of Liberty and were located only a few blocks from the World Trade Center.

He was also a member of the taoiseach's Economic Advisory Board, composed of leading Irish American businessmen, and he had many investments in Ireland, including in his native Kerry where he had purchased a spectacular home, Kenmare House.

In short, it would be hard to find a more successful Irishman anywhere in the world. Despite his rise in the world, he had never forgotten his Kerry roots and what they gave to him.

Now, on 11 September, he was returning to the US from Italy, from the isle of Capri where he, his wife Carol, son Sean and Sean's wife Wendy had attended the wedding of a member of the powerful Newhouse family. Sy Newhouse, owner of Condé Nast, the parent company of *Vanity Fair* among other publications, was a close friend.

Kelleher and his family were seated in the first class section of the Delta Airlines flight due into New York from Rome at 3.00 p.m. New York time. It had been an uneventful flight, and he was looking forward to getting back and seeing his three grandchildren again.

Suddenly, in late morning, as they approached the Canadian coast, they noticed the plane dropping sharply in altitude and commencing a sharp descent pattern. The disquiet among the other passengers was evident to Kelleher, who initially thought there was a mechanical problem with the plane. He was thus quite relieved when the captain came on to advise that there was nothing wrong with the plane, but that they had just been advised by the Federal Aviation Administration that they should land right away. He said he would give them more information when the plane landed.

There was a discernible buzz among the passengers in the plane, who were wondering what had caused the FAA to issue such a ruling. Perhaps Kennedy Airport and indeed the whole East Coast was closed by fog or there had been some kind of aviation accident, some passengers surmised.

Shortly after landing at St John's Airport, in the capital of Newfoundland, the captain came back on with an extraordinary message. "Now I can advise you that America has been invaded," he told the startled passengers. He told them that the World Trade Center had been destroyed, the Pentagon had been attacked, and that there were several other rumours of major landmarks under fire. He told them he was too emotional to discuss it any further with them but that he would find out more information on the ground and get back to them. He said no one could leave the airplane under any circumstances.

Kelleher thought he was in the middle of a bad dream. "It just seemed absurd, insane actually," he says. "How could the World Trade Center be destroyed? It was impossible, the most outlandish thing I had ever heard. And who had invaded us? I immediately thought of a nuclear missile or something like that. Everyone on board was frantic trying to find out what had happened."

His son Sean came racing over. "Dad, that's where Alex works," he said, referring to Alex Steinman, a close friend of the family. Steinman was employed in Cantor Fitzgerald, high in the north tower of the WTC.

Kelleher immediately reached for his phone. It turned out that he had the only working phone on the plane. It was a special international model that allowed him to call from or to anywhere in the world. Now as frantic passengers crowded around, he tried to raise people in New York.

Impossible. All the lines were dead, and it was clear that the catastrophe was having far-reaching consequences as attempted calls to other destinations also failed.

Finally, in desperation, with the passengers increasingly agitated, he called a lawyer in Kansas City who had recently worked on a major deal for him. Somehow the phone rang and his lawyer friend, John Marvin, picked it up.

It was from him that Denis, with the other passengers crowded around, learnt the horrific truth of what was happening in America. Marvin told him about the plane, about the unbelievable scenes of people jumping, and of buildings being levelled to the ground. "I had a very tough time comprehending what he was saying," says Kelleher.

For all the passengers on board, there was an immediate sense of shock and disbelief. For the Americans on board, the major preoccupation was their families. How were they doing, especially those resident in New York? John Marvin began calling all around the country, to relatives and friends of the passengers, relaying information when he could get it back to the plane.

Dennis found out that his son and daughter and in-laws and grandchildren were all safe. It was a tremendous moment of relief, he remembers.

Due to his company's proximity to the World Trade Center, he was also desperately worried about his employees and friends on Wall Street. However, he was unable to immediately contact them. When he did, he found out that his son's friend Alex had called his wife a number of times and told her that they were evacuating. They now had hopes that he had survived.

His own workforce had had a narrow escape. Back in Kelleher's office in New York, on the morning of 11 September, his secretary Mary Schaffer had decided to come to work early because she knew her boss was returning from his overseas trip and would want to make immediate contact. As a result, she went through the World Trade Center earlier than usual, which may well have saved her life.

When the news of the first plane hitting came over, she gathered in Denis's office with some senior executives. Suddenly they heard what proved to be the second plane, coming in overhead, with an earsplitting roar. It passed right beside them, veering sharply as it sought to hit the tower head on. They all instinctively ducked, and soon after the order to evacuate was given.

Back on the plane, having made his own calls, Kelleher's phone was getting handed around to all the news-starved passengers. Each in turn called loved ones, or anyone else if they could not get through.

Soon a relay system was set up around the country. Someone who answered in Missouri was asked to phone another family in Wisconsin where a passenger's family lived.

In such a manner, almost all the passengers on the plane were able to account for themselves and their families. When the battery on the phone ran low, they charged it from a plane outlet.

Throughout the afternoon, with the pilot at an emergency meeting, the passengers were left to fend for themselves. From the windows they could see fleets of other jets already landed on the small runway. From front to tail, Kelleher estimated there were close to 35 of the big birds on the ground. They were among the last to land, they learned. Most of the planes after them, approaching the Canadian coast, had turned around and gone back to their European points of departure.

The hours passed. Finally the captain returned and told the passengers that the "invasion" seemed to be limited to New York and Washington, that all the planes were now out of the sky and accounted for, and that the passengers were going to be taken off the plane. They would be processed by Canadian customs and kept in Newfoundland until further instructions were received. The deplaning would take place in the order of arrival, bad news for the Delta passengers. There was nothing for it but to hunker down on board, try to catch some sleep and eat the meagre remains of the food that was left on board.

At 2.00 a.m. that morning, the weary Delta passengers finally got to alight. They were tired, hungry and confused. They were warned not to take a single item off the plane except for the airline blanket. Kelleher had to leave his phone and his hand luggage on board, something that caused him understandable irritation.

Now they were taken by bus to a nearby hockey rink. There the passengers stood in line in the cold building while they were processed thoroughly by Canadian immigration agents. At 4.00 a.m. some of the passengers, including the Kellehers, were bussed to a nearby Pentecostal church to spend the night.

"They had mats on the floor, and we had to sleep shoulder to shoulder for the next six nights," says Kelleher. "To say it was uncomfortable was an understatement."

Many didn't even bother to try to sleep, preferring instead to watch CNN non-stop, their first images of what had really happened in New York and Washington. Kelleher remembers a stunned silence as they watched, over and over, the replay of the towers going down.

For Denis Kelleher and his family, the next few days would be a blur. They were just a few of 13,000 passengers stranded in Newfoundland, all in need of shelter and sustenance, and most in varying stages of shock.

Kelleher knew from his childhood history that Newfoundland had been a major settlement for the Irish almost from the time of the first emigration to the United States. It was still a surprise to find people who had never set foot in Ireland speaking with perfect Irish accents.

Newfoundland had seen its first Irish settlers in the seventeenth century, when ships from England called at several southern Irish ports to bring servants for the settlers who were setting up the first villages on Newfoundland's icy coast. A history of the period states that most of the Irish migration at first was seasonal, and that many returned. In the 1770s and 1780s, over 5,000 Irish settled there according to a local history, most from Waterford, Wexford, Carlow, Kilkenny, Tipperary and Cork.

In the nineteenth century, Newfoundland became a major emigration destination for Irish people. A local history compiled by Memorial University in St John's makes clear their influence. "They [the Irish] created a distinctive subculture that is still evident. Almost all were Catholic. Many spoke only Irish on arrival or distinctive varieties of English . . . their descendants emerged as full-fledged Newfoundlanders, a unique culture in North America."

These Irish roots ensured that Denis Kelleher and his family, and indeed all the Irish passengers who landed in Newfoundland on 11 September, received a very warm welcome.

For Kelleher, the next five days were as far removed from his busy life on Wall Street as was imaginable. "The highlight was the daily trip to Wal Mart, the department store, for clean underwear," he says with a laugh. The lowlight was trying to sleep in the cramped church with everyone lying shoulder to shoulder. "You would just be falling asleep when someone would start snoring. I don't think I slept more than a few hours over the entire period." There were other highlights though. "People invited us into their homes every night. We were told that we could shower, eat or just walk in and make ourselves comfortable. Those were wonderful people," he says.

He also got to know his fellow passengers. "We were in such close proximity that we soon knew all about each other's lives. We saw the best of people in tough circumstances, I can tell you that."

On day four, just when it looked like they might get out, the tail end of a hurricane lashed the province and they were confined a further two days. Stir craziness started to set in. The waiting was the worst part, wondering if they would be kept in Newfoundland for days, weeks even, and what was happening with their families back home. Fortunately, the Canadian authorities announced on the sixth day that the air space over New York was reopening. It was a magical moment, Kelleher recalls.

Finally, after the passengers had bid farewell to their genial hosts, the Delta plane finally took off for American airspace, to the great relief of all on board. The spirit of camraderie and friendship on board was palpable. Many have since kept in touch. "I have 300 new friends," Kelleher jokes.

For the Kellehers, the tale did not have a happy ending. Alex Steinman, so close that Denis considered him a surrogate son and Sean a brother, did not make it out of the World Trade Center, despite earlier hopes. "I gave him his first job. He was very close with my kids," says Kelleher, his voice breaking. "It was just so senseless to lose someone like that."

CHAPTER TWENTY-EIGHT

LAST MAN OUT

SERGEANT JOHN MCLOUGHLIN was working his normal beat at the Port Authority on Manhattan's West Side when the twin towers were attacked.

A veteran of the Port Authority police service, McLoughlin knew every inch of the World Trade Center and had also served in the Port Authority Emergency Service unit, created for just such an eventuality.

Married to Donna, with four kids, 15-year-old Steven, 11-year-old Caitlin, nine-year-old John and four-year-old Erin, McLoughlin and his family lived in Westchester County, the suburb north of New York City. An experienced cop, considered a true professional by his fellow policemen, he knew instinctively that he had never faced anything like what he was now heading into.

He asked two fellow Port Authority policemen, Will Jimeno and Dominick Pezzulo, to volunteer to come down with him. Both men, only nine months on the job, immediately agreed. With several other Port Authority police, they commandeered a bus and sped down the emergency lanes all the way to the WTC. The men went immediately to the north tower, which had been hit, and went under the building to get to an emergency services room filled with equipment, air masks, helmets and axes. They filled up their cart and were making their way to the disaster scene when a second huge explosion rocked the building, and they realised that a second plane had hit the south tower.

The men were in the main concourse that joined the
south tower to the north when the impact of the plane began
to collapse the walls and ceiling all around them. Suddenly a
huge fireball from aviation fuel spilling down the elevator
shaft came flying in their direction.

Desperately they ran for safety as the concourse came
down, and McLoughlin, Jimeno and Pezzulo barely made it
around a corner to avoid the fireball. Two other policemen
with them perished.

Then the walls came down. Dominick Pezzulo was
crushed in the push-up position, Jimeno's legs were completely pinned by heavy concrete, and McLoughlin was
caught worst of all, as the ceiling pinned him to the ground.
All three were trapped under the rubble, but were in a small
cavity which had allowed them to live.

They believed they had a chance, because they could see
light. The rubble was not too deep, and Officer Dominick
Pezzulo, a weightlifter, thought he could get all the rubble off
himself. After a titanic struggle he succeeded and crawled
over to where Jimeno was. Just as he began to free him, there
was a horrendous roar, and the south tower began to collapse. "It was like a huge train coming at me with the roar
of the devil," Jimeno says.

Dominick was caught by a huge cinder block, "the size
of a dining room table", that hit him across the legs. The
other two, perhaps because they were already buried, were
unscathed. Blackness descended except for a tiny ray of light
Jimeno could miraculously see high above the rubble.

Jimeno asked Dominick if he was okay. "Willy, I'm hurt
bad," he told him. Jimeno tried to keep him talking, but
Dominick went quiet. Suddenly he said "Willy, you know I
love you."

Jimeno told him he loved him, too. "Just remember me.
I died trying to save you guys," said Dominick. Moments
later he was dead.

The two men left in the blackness kept talking.
McLoughlin remembers, "I had a pretty big block of concrete trapping me . . . It was hard to concentrate on anything
other than the pain."

He felt himself slipping in and out of consciousness. He knew the rescue crews would have backed off until the following morning because the rubble was unsteady and parts could collapse at any time: "because everything was unstable and they would need daylight".

Jimeno was worried about his sergeant. He kept talking to him to keep him awake. He screamed at him: "Sarge, keep alive! You can't die on me because I'll have nobody, and I won't make it; I'm dead." Several times McLoughlin slipped into sleep, but each time Jimeno woke him up by screaming. The hours passed. Shots rang out. It was Officer Dominick Pezzullo's gun going off in the heated space. The shots missed them. They waited for someone.

David Karnes was an accountant with Deloitte and Touche in Wilton, Connecticut, a tony suburb of New York. He was also a former Marine Corps sergeant. When he saw the attack he left his office, got his Marine Corps camouflage uniform and headed for the site.

By the time he got there, the World Trade Center had collapsed, making the entire area highly unstable, and the search operation had ceased. World Trade Center 4 was burning out of control and likely to come down at any time. Karnes met another marine, a Sergeant Thomas.

Ignoring the orders to stand by, the two men began to walk over the seven-storey-high pile of rubble. As they went they called out, "United States Marines. If you can hear us, yell or tap."

No answer. It was 8 p.m., almost 12 hours after the planes had hit.

As Karnes approached the centre of the pile, Jimeno, drifting in and out of consciousness, suddenly heard him. "Over here!" he screamed.

"I heard him overhead and I said, 'Please don't leave us. This is Officer Jimeno, who has a little girl and another on the way. Sergeant McLoughlin is down here; he has four kids. Please don't leave us.'"

Karnes responded, "Buddy, I am not leaving you."

His problem was that he was alone on top of the pile, and he was unable to reach anyone because all the local phone services were dead. On his cell phone he called his sister in Pittsburgh. She phoned her local police, who got through to the New York police and fire departments, who arrived at the spot with an army of volunteers.

The key man to arrive was Charles Sereika, a medic who was among the first to the scene. Like Karnes, it was a miracle that he was there at all.

Sereika, 32, had struggled with alcoholism and had given up his paramedic's career. He had recently gone through a major rehabilitation programme. He had come back to New York sober and now went to AA every day.

When the planes hit he had grabbed an old paramedic shirt and a badge he had not used in years and hitched a ride on an ambulance down to the scene. There had been nothing to do until this call.

He was the first to the hole, and he squeezed his way down into the rubble, pushing, shoving and climbing down until finally reaching Jimeno. Sereika found he had a reasonably good pulse and sent an urgent request for oxygen and an intravenous tube. Because they were in the middle of the pile and it was getting less safe by the minute, it took a round trip of 40 minutes to get the supplies.

The other rescuers began to pry the rubble apart in order to reach the trapped man. Further down in the pile they heard Sergeant McLoughlin calling for help. There was nothing they could do until they got Jimeno out first. Two emergency service workers, Paddy McGee and Scott Strauss, squeezed down into the hole beside Sereika and began moving rubble. With Sereika stabilising him and the firemen and rescue workers digging frantically, it took them three hours to dig Jimeno free.

"Once they got the concrete off me, then I really started to feel pain," says Jimeno "I had severe compartment syndrome, a crushing injury where the body swells up and the blood has nowhere to go. I was in such pain."

But he was alive. He was carried out of the pile and strapped into a device which allowed him to be passed hand over hand through a long line of rescue workers until he was finally placed in an ambulance. He would survive. Sereika is widely credited with saving his life.

McLoughlin was thirty feet below the rescue workers after they brought out Jimeno. It took them more than eight hours to get him out of the rubble. He was in much worse shape than Jimeno. He, too, suffered compartment syndrome, except far more severely, which must be the way many survivors who were not reached died.

"They didn't know if I would make it the first night," says McLoughlin. "I had to have skin grafts on three-quarters of my body. I had no feeling in my feet or ankles." He underwent weeks of agony and a daily battle to survive. Thoughts of his family kept him going.

Amazingly, he made it through. He is now in therapy five days a week to try to strengthen his crushed muscles so he can walk again. "I can stand, and I can walk some. But I am still confined to a wheelchair. They do expect I will get feeling back," he says. "My leg muscles are so messed up that it takes every bit of strength I have just to stand. I push myself as hard as I can. It is a hard workout, but it is good, being sore. I know that my body is redeveloping again. I am much stronger than I was. I just look at it as a matter of time."

He says much of his strength comes from his family. His little daughter, Erin, loves to play doctor around him. "She helps put my brace on. Without my family support I'd be in much worse shape," he says.

He will be weak for a long time, but he has survived. He knows, too, he is among the blessed, because he was the last person out alive after the collapse.

ACKNOWLEDGEMENTS

Soon after 11 September I became determined to write about the Irish context of this massive tragedy. It was easy to find. An estimated 20 per cent of those who died were of Irish descent, more than of any other ethnic group, and the Irish in the fire and police services were particularly hard hit.

Writing the book restored my faith in the notion of heroism, and not the kind you see in Hollywood movies. So many ordinary men and women showed such selfless behaviour on that day that their bravery will never be forgotten. Far from crushing the American spirit as the hijackers sought to do, it lifted it up and gave us all a new sense of priorities about what was important in life.

Researching and writing the book should have been a gloomy task, given that so many I interviewed had lost loved ones, but I found an opposite experience. The resilience and quiet courage so many showed in the face of such tragedy touched me deeply and made me all the happier that I wrote down their stories. I owe a special thanks to all who co-operated with such dignity in the writing of this book, sometimes in very difficult circumstances for them. Inevitably there are literally hundreds of stories that are not included; it would have been an impossible task to reach out to everyone.

To all my colleagues in *Irish Voice* newspaper and *Irish America* magazine I also owe a great debt. To reporters Georgina Brennan, who researched several of the stories, to Kelly Fincham and Tom Deignan who both did invaluable research, I offer heartfelt thanks. Also, I owe a sincere debt of gratitude to Patricia Daly who introduced me to many of the subjects. I also want to acknowledge Nicola McClean whose wonderful photograph of Ground Zero appears on the book cover. A special thanks to publisher Steve MacDonogh and all at Brandon.

Finally, to my wife Debbie, for her extensive research and rock solid support right through a hectic period, a very special thank you. It would not have been possible without her.

Niall O'Dowd,
New York
July 2002

SOME OTHER READING

from

BRANDON

Brandon is a leading Irish publisher of new fiction and non-fiction for an international readership. For a catalogue of new and forthcoming books, please write to Brandon/Mount Eagle, Cooleen, Dingle, Co. Kerry, Ireland. For a full listing of all our books in print, please go to

www.brandonbooks.com

SEAN O'CALLAGHAN
To Hell or Barbados
The ethnic cleansing of Ireland

"An illuminating insight into a neglected episode in Irish history, but its significance is much broader than that. Its main achievement is to situate the story of colonialism in Ireland in the much larger context of world-wide European imperialism." *Irish World*

"A fascinating read." *Sunday Tribune*

"Essential reading." *Irish Examiner*

ISBN 0 86322 297 0

WILSON JOHN HAIRE
The Yard

Wilson John Haire entered the Belfast shipyard as an office boy at fourteen. Brought up mainly in rural areas, he was suddenly thrown into the world's biggest shipyard, a huge cauldron of twisted metal, great baulks of timber, the freezing sea, death and terrible injuries, where the day-to-day philosophy was fatalism.

"He writes very, very well. He's got a way of bringing alive a whole range of characters. There's a grinding poverty here but there's also a kind of resilience. I would recommend this." *Rattlebag*, RTÉ Radio 1

ISBN 0 86322 296 X

HENRY SINNERTON
David Ervine: Uncharted Waters

"There is not a more impressive politician in Northern Ireland than David Ervine." Senator George Mitchell

In the wake of the loyalist ceasefire of October 1994, many were surprised by the appearance, as if from nowhere, of a new, personable breed of spokesmen, who were open-minded and down-to-earth. None have impressed more than David Ervine, whose ready wit and refreshing manner have given sympathetic expression to a new unionism.

ISBN 0 86322 301 X

GERRY ADAMS
Before the Dawn
An Autobiography

"One of the most controversial but important political memoirs of recent times." *Publishing News*

"A definitive history of the Irish struggles of the 1970s, from the nationalist point of view. Adams, a fine writer, presents a straightforward, unapologetic memoir." *Publisher's Weekly*

ISBN 0 86322 289 7

MARGARET McCARTHY

My Eyes Only Look Out
Experiences of Irish people of mixed-race parentage

From Premiership footballer Curtis Fleming, to Lorna, who longed to live in America, this unique book introduces the reader to a wide variety of people of mixed-race parentage. Some are well known for high-profile achievements; most are private citizens in everyday occupations; all have their own experiences of growing up in a mostly white society.

ISBN 0 86322 284 6

DENNIS COOKE

Persecuting Zeal: A Portrait of Ian Paisley

"Stunningly insightful. . . well researched and attractively presented." *Fortnight*

"The Cooke 'report' on Paisley is reasoned and unemotional. But it is also daring in a place where sectarianism drives men to murder." *Observer*

"A rounded and authentic picture. . . A very valuable book." Eric Gallagher, *Methodist Recorder*

ISBN 0 86322 242 0